Generating Genius

Black boys in search of love,
ritual and schooling

Generating Genius
Black boys in search of love, ritual and schooling

Tony Sewell

Trentham Books

Stoke on Trent, UK and Sterling, USA

Trentham Books Limited
Westview House   22883 Quicksilver Drive
734 London Road   Sterling
Oakhill   VA 20166-2012
Stoke on Trent   USA
Staffordshire
England ST4 5NP

© 2009 Tony Sewell

First published 2009

British Library Cataloguing-in-Publication Data
A catalogue record for this book is available from the British Library

ISBN: 978 1 85856 368 8

Cover: Three of the early candidates for the Generating Genius
programme. Photo from Hackney Gazette

Designed and typeset by Trentham Print Design Ltd, Chester and
printed in Great Britain by Page Bros (Norwich) Ltd.

Acknowledgements

I am indebted to many people for their support,
encouragement and advice. The book would not have
been possible without the persistence of Gillian Klein and
the staff at Trentham Books. Elaine Lamenta for help in
Samoa. A special thanks to Oliver Clarke who believed in
me and helped me kick off Generating Genius. Thanks to
Poonam for doing the reading and all the boys in GG
family.

Contents

To Mum

1

Introduction

Genius (Latin): 'guardian deity or spirit which watches over each person from birth'

The Generating Genius programme began in 2005 as an attempt to reverse underachievement among black schoolboys and turn some into the next generation of doctors and scientists. The press release reads as follows:

> Generating Genius is a registered charity directed by UK based academic Tony Sewell and Professor Ronald Young, Pro Vice Chancellor for Graduate Studies at UWI, Mona. The programme has been operating as a summer school in Jamaica at the University of the West Indies, Mona. Once the model was perfected it was introduced into the UK. This was an example of colonialism in reverse.

The Generating Programme was slated to run for five summers to ensure that the development of those involved would be an ongoing process. An extensive programme was needed to nurture the minds of our boys, and a 'quick fix' would have been insufficient to achieve the ideal.

The programme in the UK was launched at Imperial College in London in August 2006 with the same goals of raising aspiration and achievement among African Caribbean teenage boys. The programme aims to provide incentives to boys, often from failing schools, to pursue their passion for science and to nurture talent in the community. A group of 25 boys aged 12 and 13, from London and the South East spend three intensive weeks at the College, gaining hands-on experience of science, engineering and medicine. This innovative scheme is supported by a number of the UK's top Universities.

The Generating Genius Programme focuses on four main areas: science, technology, engineering and medicine. The main objectives are:

- to guide students aged 12 onwards into a science or medicine programme at university level
- to support a sustained e-mentoring programme
- to expose students to the latest science research and practice
- to give students early exposure to the fun and responsibility of campus life

The boys are placed in groups and then compete for top prizes at the end of the summer. The groups are taught the theories and practices of each disciple and thus acquire the requisite knowledge and hands-on experience. The Generating Genius programme is not only academic but offers activities such as sports, drama, dance, music, first aid, psychological counselling, healthy lifestyles, conflict resolution, and exploring what it means to be a responsible man. Through these processes the programme seeks to develop the various academic, social and emotional skills of the boys. Generating Genius is a charity with a mission to encourage and develop under-privileged but talented black boys and have them aspire to professions in the various fields of scientific endeavour. Below is an email sent to me by one of the boys on the programme – let's call him Thomas Jackson. He attends an average but aspiring High School. His economic situation is tough, he lives with a single mother with few resources and other children. No one in his family had gone to University and few of his peers were heading in that direction. He was on the summer programme from age 12. Now 15, he is on his way to great academic achievement:

Tony,

Would it be possible to tell me whether and when there will be a project this summer. I want to do some volunteer work and work experience in the summer and I need to sort out dates that don't interfere with the project. Also I would like to know if I would be able to get the silver BA crest award maybe this summer. I got the bronze at Imperial for chemiluminescence and want the next level up. I've been looking at Cambridge University and I want to get in there so I'm trying to get 7 A*'s in GCSEs. I'm taking Chemistry, Biology, Physics and Maths in A level so again hopefully I'll get an A* and two A's.

Almost Dr Jackson

* * *

2

There are dangers in looking at success only through the lens of high academic achievement. A place at Cambridge is still the preserve of a tiny minority. What makes me passionate about Generating Genius is that the group of children we work with have been labelled the 'lost tribe' and yet, given the right attention, may well be the hidden leaders of a new generation. If this is true then it is scandalous to watch such talent go to waste. The lessons are relevant for boys who will become skilled labourers as well as Cambridge dons.

I want to make the case that black boys like Thomas Jackson do not arrive from nowhere. They were given a certain kind of parentage and patronage. There were certain kinds of inputs on their journey. The social capital possessed by certain Asian and white middle-class students is a by-product of their culture. As an educationalist, I wanted to 'generate' this culture of success amongst the group that was getting the worst results when it came to exams and school expulsions. I wanted to know what would be the right soil and fertiliser to use in the nurturing of these young males.

My thinking in the book has little time for the old style analysis of racism, not because racism has gone away but because it is not powerful enough in education systems to prevent individuals succeeding. Some of the common claims of alleged low self esteem in black children have little foundation. The classic example was that silly doll test, where black children were asked to look at a white and a black doll and say which one they preferred. Of course they would choose the white doll. I would do the same, even now. The reason has nothing to do with race and low self esteem of black children. It has everything to do with the availability of white dolls. Children like what they know. If you showed them a picture of a black woman who looked like their mother and a white woman with blond hair, they would go for the black woman who looked like their mummy.

For me the doll test is ultimately flawed. I wanted to nail the lie once and for all so I did my own doll test. But I did it not with black children but with a group of high achieving Chinese children at a local supplementary school. The toddlers came up to the table one at a time to choose between a Chinese looking doll and a white doll. Every one of these British born children of Chinese origin chose the white doll. They

3

even expressed dislike for the Chinese doll. It was proof of my theory that our over zealous African American cousins had got it wrong over the doll test. These Chinese students had chosen the white doll, not because they secretly wanted to be white. The Chinese dolls were unusual, not in the shops or featured in adverts. Yet this has not stopped Chinese children from being at the top of the academic tree. If you ask the parents why they will tell you. 'It's nothing to do with dolls stupid! It's all to do with family support'.

The white doll is not a symbol of how much I dislike myself: in post-Obama America, she is a piece of pink plastic representing nothing. I have no doubt that racism pervades society but I would have happily brought my daughter a white doll. I would happily send her to a school where she was the only black girl. Why? Because the biggest test of her self esteem is whether she had a responsible black father at home. If black children hate themselves it's because the black adults in their lives are behaving badly.

Had I been writing this book in the1960s or 1970s my analysis for success would have probably been based on new injections of blackness. It would be a text about how to resist the white institution. Things are now more complex and the successful black male has often played a game where he has had to avoid blackness (in one of its many disguises) in order to succeed. In her book *Blacked Out* (1996) Fordham speaks about successful African American males in school:

> For high-achieving African-American adolescents at Capital High warfare is the appropriate term for academic achievement because they are resisting two competing yet similarly debilitating forces: the dominant society's minimal academic expectations for black students and their classmates' internal policing for group solidarity. Among the high achieving students, resistance was manifested as conformity. They resisted dominant expectation by imagining schooling as a kind of warfare they were fighting not for themselves but for the larger, imagined Black Community, as well. (1996:235)

If young males are going into battle as good soldiers, they will need to be trained, maintained and equipped. The battle is not just about institutional racism but about a significant policing amongst themselves. To push the metaphor a bit further, black boys are also retired soldiers returning home and having to learn how to adapt to civil

4

society. This book is about the adolescent journey away from the fiery instincts to a place where they find the female within. There are lessons here for all boys.

The boys on the Generating Genius programme greatly exceeded the academic norm of their peers. We have been asking the wrong question over the years. We need to be positive and ask rather: what is the template for success for black males? How can we generate genius? What is the social ecology for black boys to succeed across the black Diaspora? These are the questions this book seeks to answer.

As I write this history is in the making, Barack Obama has been sworn in as the first black President of America. In many ways his journey through life is not too dissimilar to my own. He is my age, his father is a Commonwealth immigrant but most powerfully, he makes the journey back to the land of his father to discover his roots: in his case Kenya and in mine, Jamaica. For me, a British born black person. Jamaica would offer comfort to someone who was a stranger in the land of his birth. Obama was to discover that the Kenyan waiters, like the Jamaicans, would serve the white guests before the black. Paradise was not perfect. But it would help to give a strong sense of self. Looking back, it was Jamaican culture that helped me shape my own success. I wasn't surprised that this culture would produce a hero like Marcus Garvey, who would ultimately give African Americans their first taste of feeling big on the planet.

Obama would have seen in Kenya a place where black people could be anything, from bank manager to President. My time in Jamaica in the early eighties not only shaped and sharpened me for dealing with the racial oddity which was in Britain, but it also prepared me to reap success when better times came. I returned to my native England with 'a migrant mentality': that is, I saw only opportunity. Although both Kenya and Jamaica have terrible colonial legacies, the world seems bigger in these places outside the constraints and politics of race.

The fortune of young African and Caribbean males living in London frequently takes prominence in news and current affairs. Boys not only perform below girls in most academic disciplines – catching up only at the end of schooling and then only in Maths and Science – but they are now turning in greater numbers to crime. Students of Caribbean origin in the UK still do not reach the national average in qualifications at 16. Also prevalent is the over mothering and under fathering of many of these youths, whose young mothers struggle against often formidable odds.

My experiment began in 2005, when I took a small group of black British boys aged 12 to Jamaica and linked them with a group of Jamaican boys of the same age. We would create a science camp during the summer holidays at the University of the West Indies. This was not a football or athletics centre but a Science and Technology camp – not a discipline usually associated with black males. The boys would live for a month like University undergraduates, attending lectures, going on field-trips and encountering a life-changing experience.

The Generating Genius charity generated a swell of publicity and expectation in the press and on television as we searched for the ten lucky students who would go on this trip. We decided to have an essay competition in which students had to tell us why they wanted to be a scientist and how they would benefit from the trip. The short-listed students were interviewed, and the group chosen was unveiled in the *Voice* Newspaper as: 'Our Future'.

In Britain, America and Jamaica, educationalists and black parents were desperate for answers as to why this group was failing so badly. In Britain, it was rare to see black boys on such a high level academic venture. It was refreshing and high risk. How were these young boys going to cope in a land they knew little about? How would they get on with the Jamaican boys? Could they cope with being placed on a University campus setting at the tender age of 12?

A question of genius
The programme never intended to solve the complex problems of all black boys in one initiative, just as the election of Barack Obama never could at once free all African Americans from poverty and discrimination. But Generating Genius is important for its symbolism, its ambition and above all for its possibilities for the future. Black people in Britain needed a good news story. Here was a group of talented boys who were given an opportunity to show off their potential. It had an added value because they would be doing this with their Jamaican counterparts.

On the second day of our stay, a Jamaican lecturer came up to tell me that I was mistaken in linking these poor young boys with genius. She felt it was an overwhelming expectation which would weigh too heavily on their young shoulders. She was concerned they might be bullied by their peers, who would mock them if they knew they were being associated with the 'G' word. This lecturer saw genius as some special attribute that is bestowed on the blessed. What emerged from the Generating Genius programme was something completely different: genius equated to attitude, hard work and cultural legacy. It was ecological rather than innate so it was possible to create conditions for genius to develop. Conditions which, with understanding, attention to detail and good will, could be widely applied to the education of black boys.

Why are we talking about genius and black boys? Why can't they just be ordinary? The deliberate use of the term genius is meant to be subversive. My intention was to reinvent the notion of genius and make it more accessible, less white, less Asian, and ultimately less elitist. If we see that the reason why Chinese students are the best performing both in the UK and America has nothing to do with better innate or ethnic intelligence but everything to do with culture, it loses its elite gloss. It then becomes accessible to African American or African Caribbean boys who, as a group, score the lowest exam grades. What we need to do is radically examine the culture of black boys and provide the right cultural legacy that will give them access to the genius within.

The lessons from the 'Cane Piece'

To reach the plantation of Worthy Park, Jamaica, you take the road from Ewarton which climbs for about five miles, winding like a snake. When you come to the final ridge, you see one of the wonders of the world, a huge valley called the Vale of Lluidas.

The sugar cane is spread out for miles and the stalks bend slowly in the wind like a child clutching its belly in pain. The majestic valley is surrounded by blue-green mountains stretching back like a huge auditorium.

During the days of slavery there was a large tower at the corner of the plantation, belching out smoke as the sugar began to cook. The men and women who worked the Cane Piece were locked into a system that had them working over fourteen hours a day in the baking sun. It was hellish work with little rest time, and the whip was used on those who were unproductive.

Given the inhuman conditions, there were constant rebellions and the cane fields regularly burned. The Cane Piece was a hated space that black people desperately wanted to escape. It was the place where you sat and imagined a new world, a new time, a time when your children, like the white and brown elite, might get a decent education. It was also a place where you plotted rebellion and dreamt of a day when you could decide your own destiny.

In his book *Slaves who Abolished Slavery* (2002), Richard Hart recalls how the British put down a Cane Piece rebellion in St James, Jamaica:

> General Cotton's despatch from Montego Bay on the morning of 26th January 1832 referred to an incident at Virgin valley when the troops had made their approach on the previous day, the slaves of the estate had concealed themselves among the growing canes in a large cane-piece. Their hiding place discovered, it was set on fire but it didn't burn down. So a proclamation was sent out giving an amnesty if they would come out and surrender themselves. Only one woman took advantage of it. (2002:315)

After full Emancipation in 1838, the former slaves in Jamaica fled from the plantations and set up their own hill farms, growing their own provisions. The Cane Piece was taboo. It represented the old life. These farmers effectively ran their own businesses, juggling a family workforce and creating sophisticated systems to keep themselves and their families alive. Soon, migration would also be associated with hard work, freedom, autonomy and a better life.

In Guyana, those of African origin soon migrated from the Cane Piece to civil service jobs in the capital, Georgetown. It would be indentured farmers from East India who would take over the hated Cane Piece. These lessons served Caribbean people well, especially when they migrated to the United States, a land of opportunity which they embraced with zeal. The image of the Cane Piece gives one a positive legacy from the horrors of slavery – instead of those who peddle the notion of a black world held back by their post traumatic slave syndrome. The Cane Piece is really about resilience and creativity. It is a way of thinking that has helped those who travel to seize the opportunity to work, educate themselves and build a successful business.

Applying the lessons

Ronald F. Ferguson, a researcher at Harvard, has been surveying students at Shaker Heights High School outside Cleveland. It is an academically acclaimed school serving both white and black families, and can thus be classified as solidly middle class and upper middle class. In attempting to explain why black students perform far worse academically than their white classmates, despite similar economic backgrounds, Ferguson suggests: 'Black kids watch twice as much TV as white kids; three hours a day as opposed to one-and-a-half.'

Compare this with a significant scientific literature by Priscilla Blinco measuring Asian 'persistence'. She gave large groups of Japanese and American first graders a very difficult puzzle and measured how long they worked at it before they gave up. The American children lasted 9.47 minutes on average, but the Japanese children lasted 13.53 minutes, approximately 40 per cent longer.

Asian students in the UK and America do better than their black counterparts not because they are inherently brighter but because the cultural legacies are different. It has little to do with teacher racism or socio-economic background. The key factor is that one group is being nurtured by MTV and the other is clocking up the educational hours. This has nothing to do with innate laziness or intelligence. It simply means that black children and particularly the boys need to have greater intellectual demands made on their time. African American and African Caribbean children cannot make the link 'culturally' between hard work in a cane field or a paddie field, and social mobility. This has to be generated for them, obstacles and tasks have to be set so they can make the 'persistence' connection.

An annual event in the UK response to race and education is the London Schools and Black Children Conference. It is considered an annual diary date for those who are motivated about propelling our young people into success. The theme of the 2009 conference was exclusions (Black expulsions from school).

During the panel discussions, Diane Abbott MP and others made reference to the Priority Review report *Getting it. Getting it right*, published by the then DfES in 2007.

Pages 5 and 6 of the report provide an ethnic breakdown of exclusions for 2003/2004. For both fixed period and permanent exclusions you will see there are specific disparities between black boys. The data reveals that boys who have a Caribbean heritage are at far greater risk than boys whose heritage is African. The average for all pupils was 5.02 per cent, for black Caribbean it was 9.61 per cent and black African it was 4.43 per cent

The panel interpreted this key difference as evidence that there is specific discrimination against black boys whose heritage is Caribbean. Therefore any solutions provided by our institutions and in the community needs to acknowledge this disparity.

However, unlike those on the panel, the boys of African and African Caribbean heritage I have spoken to point not to some subtle teacher discrimination but to culture and legacy. The West African boys not only grew up under a strong patriarchy, they also had a sense of the 'Cane Piece'. They were raised with an immigrant mentality. These students, though born in Britain, see education in the same way as their parents do: as an opportunity to increase your status. African Caribbean boys lacked this legacy and relied more on their own self-determination. This was a riskier journey and many lacked the motivation and discipline to succeed in school.

In Jamaica, researchers have established a link between the unfair distribution of household chores in the home and girls' higher achievement in school. Genius has less to do with individual mental brilliance and more to do with parentage, patronage and the social ecology of the person. It is about what Malcolm Gladwell calls the 'Outliers':

> The Culture we belong to and the legacies passed down by our forebears shape the patterns of our achievement in ways we cannot begin to imagine. It's not enough to ask what successful people are like, in other words. It is only by asking where they are from that we can unravel the logic behind who succeeds and who doesn't. (Gladwell, 2008:67)

The case studies in this book show how an eco-system of success was created in the lives of the boys to allow genius to flourish. This principle underpins the creation of the science programme Generating Genius. When we returned from Jamaica, we continued summer programmes with the same group and expanded our intake. After our pilot first year to Jamaica, the decision was made not to send any more boys from the UK to Jamaica but to have separate in-country programmes. Accordingly, in the following summer Generating Genius ran a boys summer school based at the University of the West Indies and another based at Britain's top Science University, London's Imperial College. Back at school, 90 per cent of the boys on our Jamaican and UK programme have achieved significantly better academic results than their peers.

Some might say that any special attention given to students will produce a positive result. I would say yes and no. If we look at the students who have been showered with special attention, special funding, mentors, role models and attending conferences, the result has been only a slight improvement. What counts is the *kind* of special attention that is applied. Some initiatives work and others are irrelevant. This book will hopefully save governments and education boards large sums of money by forestalling interventions that are a waste of time, such as efforts to purify schools and teachers of institutional racism.

Teachers in hard-pressed classrooms may well feel that they do not have the luxury to work with their students in the same way we connected with the Generating Genius boys. This is a fair point. But what we have uncovered in this work are the underlying principles that seem to bring black boys success.

People have failed to listen to the cries of black boys in the UK and in America. Researchers who have their own political agenda have attempted to make the data fit their theory. In the face of male violence within black communities, they are silent. They have no answer when black boys say they are the victims of enormous peer pressure.

Genius is not something sent down by God (although it helps). It is really all about opportunity. If IQ scores alone are not the determining factor for success, then surely a good state education programme should be giving students opportunities to succeed?

During our Summer Generating Genius programme where 12 year old black boys lived on University campus away from the comfort zone of home, their true natures were revealed. The boy who probably had the highest IQ of all was the one who was eventually told to leave the programme. Like the rest of the students, he came from an economically poor background, but he had the good fortune to go to one of the top schools in his area. But he didn't fit. The loss or exclusion of students from a programme does not mean that the programme is poor. It just means that the boy did not pass our test.

What we had indirectly created was a rite of passage. Traditional societies would feel comfortable with a programme that took adolescent boys away from their mothers and put them in the woods to fend for themselves for a month. This was not a form of child abuse, it was a message to boys that becoming a male was another kind of birth. It would take courage to succeed.

Ritual, love and schooling

The Generating Genius programme was immensely challenging. But the boys who pursued it found themselves supported within a stable triangle made up of ritual, love and schooling. Each concept had specific application, as described below.

Ritual

Our ancestors had a practical problem, a problem that troubles politicians today. How do you control the testosterone-driven young males in the community? Youths had the potential to tear down the village and rape all the women. And the older men wanted to maintain their power and control over the females. They didn't have an Ethnic Minority Achievement Grant or Sure Start but there *were* creative rituals: the myths and rituals that tell a man who he is and what he values. By composing his religion (from the Latin religere = to bind back) they bind him back through memory to divine ancestors who call upon him to act and think in certain ways. They also bind back those powerful instincts that will destroy civil society.

In a cynical and scientific age it is hard to speak of these matters without being positioned as a new age primitive. However, it is actually around the crisis of boys' achievement and behaviour that we hear the ancestors' voices in the background.

As Kindlon and Thompson remark: 'Good discipline contains a boy and his energy, providing a sense of physical and emotional security he needs in order to learn the larger lessons of self-control and moral behaviour (1999:34)'. In her book *About our Boys* (2007), Lucinda Neall writes:

> Wrestling is a useful way for boys to learn and practise self-defence whether or not a boy actually needs this skill later in life ... Many boys benefit from the discipline of martial arts, such as Tae Kwondo, Karate or boxing. These calm aggressive boys and give confidence to quieter boys. (Neall, 2007:48)

Our programme was secular and made no noises towards any religions. However once you look at ritual, you have to explore ideas of how traditional societies reared its young men. The chaos spoken of in the Bible is just another way of talking about masculine instincts let loose. Any civil society should have a grasp of the old legends and stories which talk of man's struggle with the gods and his own hubris. We begin to link the teaching of Science with the study of Greek and Latin – not for snob value but as a guide for boys to understand their own masculinity. Take that wonderful myth of Icarus and Daedalus: the son decides to use the wings to fly, ignores his father's advice and flies too close to the sun. His wings melt and he comes crashing down to earth. This is a great story about father and son, about role models and about the male ego.

The use of Greek and Latin classic stories affords opportunities not only to unpick the struggles of black masculinity, but also to learn much from the language. Ethnologists agree that man everywhere first meets the divine as that which animates the world, provides its zest, sparkle, energy, power, oomph – that invisible something that distinguishes the quick from the dead and the vivid from the dull. Our boys began to research the word 'animates' and found it came from *anima*, Latin for soul or breath (corresponding to the Greek psyche) and if man's soul is his breath, then the world's soul is God's breath, the wind, the breath of life. We then linked this to the Greek word *phusis* = Nature and this it is akin to phusao = to blow and phuo = generate or grow.

This is when teaching and learning get really exciting: we can go back to our African ancestors on the savannah and understand how they linked a light wind rustling through the trees with the rising and falling of the chest, rising and falling with the breath of life – the first notions of divinity. The idea that man's soul is his breath is very old indeed, as old as the creation stories in which man is fashioned of clay and life breathed into him by gods.

There need be no conflict between the creation stories and science. They needed each other, one to tell us how and the other to tell us why. The penny dropped for our boys when they said, 'well, that means every time we breathe we become like gods'. It meant we could have a serious discussion about pollution and the environment. And we could talk about masculinity and civil society, for we could see divinity as something that 'pollutes' the person in contact with it unless his exposure is regulated by the laws of taboo. As one boy perfectly put it: 'So sir the reason why we have so much knife crime is down to bad breath.'

The matter of the imagination and dreaming is important. Even in ancient Egypt and Greece, where the mastery of astronomical mathematics was astonishingly sophisticated, pharaohs and other men of substance would retire when in trouble to sacred compounds in the hope of a dream to direct their actions. Were these men wrong, 'primitive' in the bad sense? I say no. Serious dreams make a greater impression than most of our waking experience, so commonsense suggests they matter. For those from an African Caribbean background, dreaming and re-telling dreams was a wonderful source of story-making and telling. Many of us have had a portentous dream at a time of crisis, that reflected the state we were in and offered, however obscurely, to clarify our confusion. Only our belief about the 'subjectivity' of dreams prevents our agreeing with primitive man that 'breath' might offer glimpses of how these inner instincts stir our depths with the energies of love and war. The pharaohs could agree to this without offending their reverence for astronomical mathematics: why can't we? We were teaching the science of how things work alongside the 'science' of feelings. That's what the ancient Egyptians and Greeks did in their academies. The gods and their stories were invented so that young men, in particular, could bind back the warring instincts and prevent chaos. In an age where they disproportionately fill our prisons and mental institutions, black males are hungry for such guidance.

Detractors may well say that studying Greek and Latin is too white or Eurocentric, forgetting that Greek culture was heavily influenced by the older cultures of Egypt and the Middle East. What makes the ancient Greeks work for black boys is the profound knowledge they had of masculinity.

14

There is much talk about role models and the channelling of energy. What is clear is that rituals are about actions, be they a walkabout in the woods or a birthday celebration to mark a boy's coming of age. We have watched across the black diaspora as gangs have stepped ahead of civil society, providing our young men with much needed rituals – such as initiation rites in which a boy is asked to earn his membership by committing a violent crime. The gangs provide much needed role models or father figures and they know that crime can be one way of burning up boys' energy. Nineteen teenagers died in 2008 in London alone as the result of violent attacks.

We cannot leave our children, like those in Golding's *Lord of the Flies*, to develop their own rites of passage. Generating Genius is an example of a modern ritual, by which boys can safely make the journey across to manhood, supervised by caring adults who understand their needs.

Love

'What's love got to do with it?' goes the song. Well, everything really. Whilst I was working with children who would be considered as gifted and talented, it became clear to me that many of them not only lacked social skills but also found it hard to receive kindness and love. What many of these students had in common, particularly boys of mixed heritage, was a fear of male authority. In fact, as a leader of black boys, I found myself having problematic relationships with several boys – all without a father at home – who found it difficult to accept my authority. I soon began to question my own practice. Was I too harsh with boys like these? Should I turn a blind eye to their bad behaviour because the males in their lives have been problematic?

John Eldredge asserts that 'Masculinity is bestowed. A boy learns who he is and what he's got from a man, or in the company of men; he cannot learn it any other place' (2001:34). A rather strong statement, and I can hear some feminists crying 'sexism'. However Eldredge is right to point out the real differences that exist in the way in which a man loves his son or how women love boys. I must define what I mean by love here: I am talking of caring fatherly love that has no sexual content. Eldredge speaks of how men enjoy action activities with boys, whereas a mother, but not all women, will connect with boys for who they are. Lucinda Neall (2007) describes this male love well:

15

Men can involve boys in their own interests and activities, and introduce them to the things they themselves used to like to do as boys. A lot of boys just like hanging out with men, watching and helping. When a man shares what he loves with a boy – music, sport, wildlife, fishing, computers, reading – he is giving part of himself to that boy. Sport can provide a great common interest and strong bond between males. If you don't like the same sports as the boy, if one of you is sporty and the other is not, or you don't share each other's interests, then look for something new you can do together. (2007: 182)

In *Wild at Heart,* Eldredge tells of a time he took his sons Sam and Blaine rock climbing. Sam got stuck at an overhung and his dad offered to lower him down on the rope:

'No,' he said 'I want to do this,' I understood. There comes a time when we simply have to face the challenges in our lives and stop backing down. So I helped him over the overhang with a bit of boost, and on he went with greater speed and confidence... As Sam ascended I was offering words of advice and exhortation. He came to another challenging spot, but this time sailed right over it. A few more moves and he would be at the top. 'Way to go, Sam. You're a wild man.' He finished the climb, and as he walked down from the back side I began to get Blaine clipped in. Ten or fifteen minutes passed, and the story was forgotten to me. But not to Sam. While I was coaching his brother up the rock, Sam sort of sidled up to me and in a quiet voice asked, 'Dad, do you really think I was a wild man up there?'

Miss that moment and you'll miss a boy's heart forever. It's not a question – it's *the* question, the one every boy and man is longing to ask. Do I have what it takes? Am I powerful? Until a man knows he is a man he will forever be trying to prove he is one, while the same time shrink from anything that might reveal he is not. Most men live their lives haunted by the question, crippled by the answer they have been given. (2001:90)

Ivan Congreve, who runs the Salvation Army's Springfield Lodge, said that some boys joined gangs as an alternative to their own family: 'All of our guys are from a broken family of one sort or another and that leads them into gangs'. Springfield Lodge provides men aged 16 to 21 with a home and teaches them the skills to become independent.

Ironically, there is much evidence to show that gangs and their leadership understand boys' need for love so provide an alternative love. It is within the gang that too many boys in the black diaspora find a loving caring family. Many of the young men do have relationships with their mother and father but they see them as 'mates' rather than parents, Mr Congreve said. 'They would go to them to get something but not for advice. They haven't built up a relationship with them.' He told the BBC:

> We are set in between Peckham and Brixton. We have a lot of gang culture in the area. That's where they seem to be able to find the family they are looking for. They are accepted, looked after and respected in ways that they don't feel they get from their family. Although a gang is quite a dysfunctional family, they still see it as a family. (BBC World News, March 2007)

This book unravels how we can learn from the perverse loyalty and love offered by gangs and use the boys' desire to connect positively and engage them. This is the tough love that I offer to my own community, a love that has not been undertaken by the education and social research community.

Schooling

The third ingredient for resilience relates to schooling and this is the focus of the case studies and much of the book. I have already questioned the link between Institutional racism and black educational underachievement. Take, for example, research carried out at the University of Warwick in England which examined the profile of pupils entered by teachers to take higher-tier papers in their maths and science tests at 14. Pupils can only get top marks by sitting these papers, and the tests determine the range of GCSEs they can go on to take.

White pupils were found to be significantly more likely to be entered for the top tiers than their black Caribbean, Pakistani, black African and Bangladeshi classmates. Most of the differences were explained by the pupils' previous results or by other factors which might have put them at a disadvantage, such as their economic status entitling them to free meals, the level of education reached by their mothers, and truancy and exclusion – all strong predictors of academic performance. But for a significant proportion of black Caribbean pupils, there was no academic explanation for their being excluded from the harder papers.

The researcher, Steve Strand stated that, 'After accounting for all measured factors, the under-representation is specific to this one ethnic group and indicates that, all other things being equal, for every three white British pupils entered for the higher tiers, only two black Caribbean pupils are entered.' He concluded that institutional racism and low expectations by teachers explain the discrepancy, explaining that by 'institutional racism' he meant: 'organisational arrangements that may have disproportionately negative impacts on some ethnic groups'. But he added that other research suggests that teachers' judgment of academic ability could be warped by pupils' behavioural problems:

> It is widely perceived that black Caribbean pupils are more confrontational. The question is, how much is real behavioural problems and how much is a problem between teachers and pupils. Teachers might say it is about pupils' behaviour. Black Caribbean parents will say it's teachers prejudicing against their kids. Others say behavioural issues are a response to low expectations from teachers ... To break the cycle, the best policy lever we have is with the teachers. (*Guardian* on line, September 5 2008)

Strand's research was heralded as incontrovertible evidence that African Caribbean children were the victims of institutional racism. What was missing from the research was the fact that education achievement is not about innate ability but mostly about hard work. The reasons why African Caribbean boys are less likely to be entered into top tiers is because they are not working as hard as their white peers.

The teachers cannot take the risk on individuals who will fail the harder exam. The only evidence they have is whether the student has made the effort throughout the year. Poor behaviour and attitude is a valid reason for doubting the ability of a student to perform in an exam. This is splendidly articulated by former UK television Multicultural Commissioning Editor Farrukh Dhondy, who wrote in the *Times Educational Supplement* in 1999 about the need to look wider than institutionalised racism in schools to find the cause of Black underachievement:

> The other possibilities need a hard and scientifically passionate examination. It has never been done. Instead we have notions about 'culture', 'role models', 'stereotyping', 'positive images,' 'low expectations' and 'unwitting racism' floating about which are grasped from the latest fashionable ethos and put into play in every circular discussion of the wretched subject ...

He goes on:

> Doesn't any institution want to draw up some correlative tables about class conditions, family conditions, details of parenting, cultural pursuits at home,

amount of homework done, behaviour in class, voluntary attention spans, respectful and polite behaviour, however animated or lively, and the great goal of achievement? (*Times Educational Supplement*,1999:6)

In response to the Warwick research I wrote:

We have left a generation of students to flounder without guidance. The Warwick University research is irresponsible. It not only undermines hard-working teachers but it makes our students articulate victims. Liberal researchers have positioned black pupils as being on the spectrum of child abuse, in a world where adults can never be trusted.

To tackle this issue needs an honesty that demands more from black pupils and their families. The irony is that the low expectations of too many social science researchers has left us lacking any intelligence on why black pupils fail and how to solve it. Instead they refuse to ask the hard questions of the pupils themselves and so get the answers they already expect. (*Guardian*, September 5 2008, p9)

This book argues not for de-schooling but for more schooling. There is evidence across the black diaspora that black boys are clocking up less education time than their sisters and other ethnic groups. To describe this as institutional racism is too extreme. It is a cultural legacy gap that needs to be bridged by the family, the school, the child and the wider community. It means looking at the notion of schooling more imaginatively, and that does not just mean more time in the formal classroom. Rather, we should also be talking about educational social capital, which includes gap years, summer schools and after-school opportunities.

The road leads to resilience

Good love, ritual and schooling together endow boys with resilience: the capacity to rebound and adapt successfully in the face of adversity. Resilience helps children develop social competence, problem-solving skills, critical consciousness, autonomy, and a sense of purpose. The concept of resilience grew out of recognition by clinical psychologists, psychiatrists, and others interested in child development that the term 'at-risk youth' was based on a negative view of young people and failed to recognise and appreciate their strengths and individuality. Risk factors are defined as variables that increase the probability of bad outcomes but a merely statistical concept of risk provides no information about the underlying processes.

It has been argued that the resilience black boys need collapses because they do not have access to enough positive black history and culture. The argument is also used as a justification for having separate black schools. Even though Generating Genius was targeting African Caribbean boys, this was not a withdrawal programme. It was a community based holiday time activity which supported boys to be strong and resilient in their multi-ethnic daytime schools.

For the purposes of the project – and this book – resilience is focused on children at risk of adverse developmental outcomes. It is built on specific factors such as children's competence being developed as a strength. Researchers have found that many young people who lived in high-risk situations overcame risks. Studies of at-risk children led quickly to the recognition that certain children did not succumb in the same way as others do to maladaptive behaviour. Such children seemed to be in some way protected against the negative effects of parental, social or environmental factors so that their development could proceed apparently unimpaired by difficulty. Black boys need to have less excuses made on their behalf and to be given more opportunities to fortify their characters. This will be done when they are given programmes, particularly during adolescence, that challenge the body, mind and soul.

To suggest that race and racism play no significant role in the lives of black boys would be totally naïve. However, this generation of young males seem able to withstand it. What seems to be a tougher challenge is withstanding the pressures from home and the peer group. Generating Genius is an illustration of what can be done.

This is explored in the next chapters. They set the context for the Generating Genius project: why it was needed and the forms it took. Chapter 2 looks at the family patterns of African Caribbean boys in the UK and analysis how they affect the boys' academic performance and life chances. Chapter 3 outlines the role of history in black male sexuality and the attraction of gang culture, but it also indicates ways in which boys can find the female within.

The picture is enriched by the two case studies that follow. They describe the sustained initiatives that have changed the lives of boys in a secondary school in Samoa, and in a primary school in a poor part of

Jamaica. The final part of the book is devoted to the Generating Genius Project: its aims, operation and outcomes.

Four years on and ninety per cent of the boys are on target to achieve ten excellent GCSEs, which puts them in the top ten percentile for their age. Their school reports have consistently been good to excellent and all have ambitions to attend top flight universities in the UK. Set up to tackle the transatlantic problem of the underachievement of black pupils, the programme sought boys who had genuine potential and aspirations to achieve entrance to higher education in various competitive disciplines such as Medicine, Science and Engineering. The outcomes were significantly positive: the boys not only achieved higher grades than predicted but showed greater maturity and leadership than their peers. Ritual, love and schooling had had the desired effect.

2

Fatherless boys

Our Father who art in heaven hallowed be thy name. *The Lord's Prayer*

(Sung)
It was the third of September; that day I'll always remember,
'cause that was the day that my daddy died.
I never got a chance to see him;
never heard nothin' but bad things about him.
Mama I'm depending on you to tell me the truth.

(Spoken)
Mama just looked at him and said, Son,

(Sung)
Papa was a rollin' stone.
Wherever he laid his hat was his home.
And when his died,
All he left us was alone. *The Temptations*

African Caribbean and African American families have always been dysfunctional – though no more, dare I say, than the British Royal family. It could even be argued that the centuries of disruption caused by slavery and colonialism have forced Caribbean people to think particularly imaginatively about how to raise children. Fathers have largely been replaced by aunts and grandmothers. Men have had to raise children not from their seed. Children have called non-blood relatives Aunt and Uncle. The idea that the break-up of black families led to moral decline and delinquency is questionable. What it did mean was that children were raised by extended families and the wider community.

23

This pattern continued with the migration of workers from the Caribbean to Britain in the 1950s. Men went ahead for work in Britain and later sent for their wives and then their children. The children initially left behind were often raised by grandmothers in rural Jamaica and eventually came to Britain as teenagers, where they had to get to know their parents whom they had last seen when they were toddlers.

The absent mother and father has been a feature of African Caribbean life since slavery. The attraction of overseas or urban labour has left children having to adapt to a range of carers, usually within their communities. In Jamaica they have even invented a name for this dysfunction, calling the children 'barrel children'. These are children left behind in Jamaica with a grandmother, aunt or friend while the parent goes abroad to work. A barrel of goods or money is then sent back to these children. Recent studies have shown that many barrel children feel emotionally isolated, some become disruptive in school and some boys are led on to a pathway of crime.

Since the late twentieth century, an on-going debate has raged over the extent to which a new generation, particularly boys can cope with the absence of their father. What is the real impact on the development and attitudes of African Caribbean boys of being raised by single mothers?

Four factors have made the absence of fathers a more complex problem than in the past. First is the lack of extended families in the UK. Secondly, the steady decline of male adult authority has been largely undermined by an increasing agenda around child abuse. Third is the new economic independence of black women in Britain, who are able to fund a household without the income of a male partner. Fourthly, the availability of welfare and housing provided to single working-class mothers has indeed lessened the risk of or need for putting up with flaky men.

The result has been that a new generation of African Caribbean males have been raised without the permanent presence of their father. The link between an absent dad and the disproportionate number of boys excluded from school was carefully avoided by the dominant liberal educational discourse. Instead the blame was placed mainly on white teachers and institutional racism. There has been little literature in the UK on the key correlation between fatherhood and the academic performance of young black males.

If Black boys are disproportionately 'naughtier' in schools than other pupils because they lack the restraining hand of a father then what can we as a community do? These are tough questions that our community should have faced long ago. Instead, we avoided them. It was too easy to allow white liberal scholars and black nationalists to blame everything white. This stuck way of thinking has to be challenged if anything is to change.

The sins of the fathers

Fatherhood and its absence is key to understanding the crisis facing many, though not all, black boys in the UK. This is not to deny the deliberate positioning of black males by and in a society that still loathes and envies black masculinity. However, we are doing something to ourselves and too often it happens to be another version of envy and loathing. To what extent does the absent father help us to understand these self-destructive elements?

From the infant boy's point of view, a father is at first a less immediate figure. The mother is all around him while he is inside her but once he is born, this experience is gradually diluted by the entrances of other people, adults and older children, who take over from time to time. The speed of this process varies greatly, but the direction does not. The luckiest children get to know their father as an intimate early on. Most cultures tell us that the sexes are opposite so it comes as a surprise for new parents to discover that the infant requires more or less the same kind of care from both. Men experience hormonal changes when their partners have babies. A fall in testosterone makes them more maternal. Yet the differences, however small, are significant. The father never had his child inside his body and he does not have to give much, in terms of volume of genetic material and of time, to produce him. He does not even have to survive until the child is born.

Babies have little concept of gender at birth but usually develop an identification with the mother, since she is the primary caregiver. To the others around him gender is of enormous importance and the little boy soon discovers that he is male, which is not the same sex as his mother. 'Disidentification', a term coined by Greenson (1968), is the painful process of becoming 'not female', a repudiation of femininity which is a familiar feature of most boys' development. 'I am not like her', he thinks;

25

but then; 'who am I like?' What follows thereafter is the need for identi-fication with masculinity (see Frosh *et al*, 2001). This is an uneven journey for most boys, who will make exaggerated efforts at being superman at one moment and become helpless infants the next.

The extremes of superman and infant is key to understanding some of the development issues of young black males. During the early days of Generating Genius, we interviewed boys as part of the selection pro-cess. One of the questions we asked was: 'what would you like to be-come when you leave school.' In nearly 70 per cent of the cases we got the response: 'A professional footballer'. These boys were in fantasy land – many of them could barely kick a ball. Many lacked the maturity to see themselves outside of the superman world of a football star.

A girl's identification, if smoother, is more complex because she has to distinguish herself from the mother's person but not from her gender. Paternal functions are just as important for girls, but that is another topic.

It is this process of disengagement with the 'female', that I am arguing is fundamental to understanding what has gone wrong for many black boys in the UK, North America and the Caribbean. In order to get to grips with some of these complex processes, the best place to turn is to mythic stories. This is how our ancestors would communicate pro-found ideas and we need to revive some of these tales in order to give a framework to the confusion and noise that surrounds us.

Masculinity, and the male initiation rites that signify maturation, are in every culture defined by being Not Feminine. In the film *300*, about the making of the Spartans, boys aged 13 are seen being forcibly pulled away from their screaming mothers to be placed alone in the wild woods for months. Most of them would not come back alive.

Much of Homer's *Odyssey* is about the tension between the female and masculine hero: the story of the man who is a war hero and now must make the journey home. Along the way he is tested by the gods and en-counters adventures and distractions. It could be argued that the story explores the male mindset that underpinned patriarchy even then, by presenting varieties of the feminine – the nubile (Nausicaa), sexually predatory and matriarchal (Calypso, Circe), politically powerful (Arete), domineering (the Laestrygonian King's huge daughter and mountainous wife), monstrous and all-devouring (Scylla, Charybdis), seductive and lethal (the Sirens), and the loyal, domesticated and maternal (Penelope).

The new irony is that in order to tackle female obstacles you will need 'female' strategies. This is the new dispensation where men will have to understand the Chinese concept of yang (male) and yin (female). The Chinese terms both cancel and preserve the gendering tendency, and remind us that there is no yin without yang, and that an excess of one always calls for redress from the other. In other words both male and female have yang and yin within them.

For African Caribbean boys the necessary process of ejecting the 'female' is done by themselves or with the assistance of other fatherless boys. It is messy, dangerous and in too many cases, self-destructive. Good fathers (and lucky mothers) understand that in becoming masculine you have to hold on to both the female and male aspects of yourself. You need to use your strong right arm at the same time as you learn how to cuddle and caress. In educational terms you need to have language, intellect, the ability to plan, and more importantly, the ability to socialise. These are key 'female' qualities that need to be retained by the new male hero. For me, the test for Odysseus was whether he could compete in a world where a strong right arm was less of an advantage than a nurturing left arm. The problem facing all our boys is that we're instinctively tooled up to go to war. In the past it was the role of our fathers, who best understood these matters, to put a brake on these instincts by providing distractions, rituals, rites and lawlines to hold back those young bucks.

Traditional fathers came into their own when the child was older. For sons this was also the shift from mother's apron strings to an apprenticeship with father and his craft. In the modern world the presence in a small boy's daily life of real men, as opposed to stereotypical heroes in cartoons and stories, will help him to find a more balanced sense of gender (Pruett, 1993). The term 'role model' is often applied here, but it is inadequate. Identification is much more than imitation. A famous footballer may be a role model, but real identification can only be acquired through personal contact. The boy needs a rounded character, not a cardboard cut-out.

Even when black boys appear to be doing well, a good father figure can be a help or a hindrance. This is particularly true in West African families, where elders are given such high status. This interview with a London College student of Nigerian parentage shows, however, that even when the father is present he can still be a negative force. Dotun is the lonely inner-city achiever and the distant father may have high expectations of his son but has not given him the channels to share his doubts and frustrations:

> The best way to describe my life… I'd say it's complicated. I come from a very successful family and seeing that I'm the first born I can understand why there is pressure on me to achieve, not necessarily from my mother however. Every time I do an exam, the first thing I think of is always what my parents say if I don't do too well. I almost don't even want to talk about it, or sometimes I'll say I did good to relieve myself of the stress. It's not like I'll get into trouble for doing bad, but I just don't want to face my dad. I'm not afraid of him; it's just that talking to him about my education can be really annoying.

> I'm usually very quiet in my house, being in my bedroom by myself most of the time. My dad usually asks me what the matter is but I simply say nothing to avoid talking to him. He says I can talk to him about anything, but with me that's not the case. I feel that people do not understand me that I'm different, and I do not fall into the youth stereotype. In a sociology lesson with Mr Wilson we were asked to tick the deviancies and crimes we have done throughout our life. Apparently, scoring only two out of 46 offences for me seemed impossible to believe to the others as I am a young black boy. In college I'm even quiet. In lessons teachers may ask questions to the class. I may know the answer but I don't say anything. I'm not scared or intimidated however. Even during breaks I avoid socialising with friends and spend my time in the library because I'm very independent.

> Where I live has not affected me either. There tends to be a lot of crime where I live, and that comes back to why I wear certain clothes. I don't want to get involved in the stuff others do and I don't want to be a victim. While I'm out during college, sometimes I do not return home until 5.45pm. My parents sometimes wonder if I've been doing anything else and I say no. Sometimes I feel ashamed because if they knew me really well they'd know I wouldn't do that stuff – hanging around on the street with friends at night, causing trouble etc. I dislike being outside the house in the night for a long period of time if I'm alone or with my brother.

Sometimes I talk to my brother about issues such as events at school and such, but I still do not talk to him about issues like the ones I've explained. My family does call me weird at times, but I don't mind, because it's true.

People believe in a family you are free, but I don't. There are still things that you are required to do. When my dad returns I feel 'forced' to say hello while it comes naturally to my mother. I do not know when I will be 'free'.

Some people know me as a lively, funny guy and a quiet boy. If I'm quiet it annoys others somehow, because I'm not lively, but I'm not here to benefit them. Well, I try to be nice; I don't like having people dislike me. A few people have often called me sensitive and 'different'.

I even worry about my grades. Sometimes I think I am not that well equipped for the next level. People often call me smart, but this is not the case. I know how to prioritise so studying and completing tasks is quite easy. However I still complete tasks closer to the deadline. During primary school and SATS I did very well, but from GCSE things started slipping. I worry if I'm to get an AAB or even AAA at the end of the year. Teachers say I worry too much. I have gone in several exams feeling confident, but the result is not what I expected. History for instance, a U grade. That is a whole year wasted, and does not even contribute to my total UCAS points.

I wish I had an older brother. My dad asks me if it's to avoid responsibilities, but this isn't true. I want to have guidance, but I feel this is something no-one can help me with. If they truly knew the way I act, feel etc. then I feel I can make a great progress.

I do not feel I am successful, at least not yet. If I am able to become a well qualified barrister then yes, I would say I have been successful. Then again, will I live long enough to achieve what I want?

I dislike talking to people about these things because they will get a different picture of me. I'd prefer it if they would just not know.

Sometimes I feel like I'm not raised properly. My parents are telling me things which they should tell me when I'm 9 or 10. So sometimes I feel like a baby rather than an 18 year old. It's sometimes humiliating in public and I feel un-intelligent.

When I get results people are eager to know. When I tell someone I got a C, they say it's good – it isn't. Others will ask why I got it because they feel I can do much better.

People say I look like my dad. I dislike that. I do not think that is a good thing. Of course, I'm not saying he's unattractive or along those lines, but I dislike being compared to him. If I grow up to be like him, it's like the whole thing is just repeating itself.

Although I can get upset at my little sister for doing certain things, I'm still happy that I've got a girl in the family. I don't think anyone realises this but it's a fact.

I thought Dotun's account was rather sad. Clearly, achievers have to go through much personal angst to do well. Girls have a different pressure – they are expected to do well. Dotun is clearly struggling to live in a masculinity that is different than the norm for black males. His concern about looking like his Dad reveals a lot. Most boys who have a positive relationship with their fathers are happy to know they resemble him. The culture has made it hard for him to connect with his father, yet he still desires a father figure to love him. African Caribbean fathers may statistically be more absent than their African counterparts but the distant father figure may be just as bad as the absent father. The stern father image is tough for a boy who clearly needs a hug from his old man.

Role models

As black communities in the UK struggle to replace the father figure, the mantra of role model is heralded as the new solution. In 2007, the government announced that 'successful role models for young black men' were to be recruited to counteract educational underachievement and the influence of gang culture. The search was be led by entrepreneur Tim Campbell, the first black winner of the television programme, The Apprentice. He was to hunt for 20 men – doctors, lawyers and businessmen. The Black Boys' National Role Models programme boldly claimed be an 'antidote to a culture of low aspiration'.

But the cry for more positive black role models in response to the underachievement of black children just plays to a cliché. The evidence shows that when you roll out these people the only real beneficiaries are the role models themselves. The problem is that children, black or white, need exposure to experience and authenticity. The role model who comes to the assembly and waxes lyrical about his own experience is usually forgotten by playtime.

It could be argued that one reason for the success of Generating Genius is down to my own role as loving patriarch. I had deliberately constructed a role which would allow the boys in both the UK and Jamaica to respect and also fear me. At first I was uncomfortable in this role but I sustained it because the boys seemed to like it. I was Mr High Expectations, who would boot them off the project if they dared mess up.

My rationale for this came from my days as an inner-city school teacher, where boys seemed to have the greatest love and respect for the strictest teacher. These men and women were not abusive; they actually cared for the children. They would be the ones who would challenge a student, not ignore him, if they saw him doing wrong. They would find the energy and time to stay behind and keep children in detention rather than go home and relax. The boys on the Generating Genius project were all contemptuous of the teachers who allowed them to get away with bad behaviour, but they spoke highly of those who drew lawlines around them. These teachers were different from staff who were bullies or 'shouted' at them. There was no doubt that I had constructed a father-figure about whom these boys had certain expectations.

The greatest challenge to my fatherly role came from boys who had no father at home. That said, many boys who were brought up by their mums did not find my role problematic. Those who did were deeply worried when I corrected them for their bad behaviour, quickly bursting into tears and looking terrified. I realised that my Zeus-like persona was really too tough for these children. The problem was that any slippage into my female side would confuse them.

It soon became clear that all this was nothing to do with my clever acting and everything to do with the fact that I am an adult black male. The boys in question were of a mixed-heritage background and the black males in their lives were absent and unreliable. What was emerging was a picture where few really knew any black men who acted as a stable father figure. For these boys any black man coming into their lives on this intimate level would be like the ghost returning. Of course they would have problems with me because I represented that which rejected them in their past.

Recent studies seem to support the traditional sequence in which father becomes more important after the age of 10 or 11 (Lamb and

Lewis, 2004; Steele and Steele, 2004) but this turns out to be dependent on early intimate contact between father and child. The Steeles found that fathers who have not understood their own life stories and have not mourned their losses are less engaged as parents. These men are more passive in their thinking and their children less confident and sociable. This is true in many black communities where the cycle of father-need seems to pass from generation to generation.

The real difference between fatherhood and flaky role model schemes is the marking of lawlines. These lines have sacred power. They are the ones children understand, just as the lines they avoid when walking on the pavement. To step on these deadly tramlines would mean certain bad luck and perhaps a horrible death.

Does this mean that boys respond better than girls do to lawlines? Yes, men are generally more disposed than women to play by the rules. The usual explanation draws on the history of hunters who follow set sequences. Under patriarchal systems boys handle sharp tools and play more games at school than girls do, and success in the workplace comes from observing the rules or conventions of the local game; whereas female success in the getting and nurturing of infants calls on other talents.

The post-modern academic may find this idea offensive. However, in Generating Genius we had plenty of boys who responded to the world as individuals but all the boys showed a desire for a father-figure who would give them lawlines. The variety within black boyhood is acknow-ledged but there are some core factors that the group had in common. What's more, when the rule-making male wants a serious innings with his anarchic instincts, he declares war on his neighbour, thereby legiti-mising a good deal of mayhem without disturbing his sense of himself as one who bows to the law.

Grossman and her colleagues (2002) show how fathers in conventional families, where it is the mother who spends more time with the chil-dren, have a unique role in helping them to explore the wider world from the secure base the mother provides. Feldman (2003) highlights a specific connection between fathers and baby boys. She notes the gender differences in the rhythms of intimate contact that make fathers are more in tune with sons, and mothers with daughters. 'The coregulation formed between father and son during the first months may be essential environmental inputs that facilitate the formation of self regulatory capacities' (p17). Father's attentive care of his baby son seems helpful in its own right, not just as an adjunct to mother's.

Babies thrive when they have several familiar and loyal caregivers so they don't have to have an exclusive relationship with only one. This was the real strength of the early African Caribbean extended family in both the Caribbean and the UK.

There are of course many lone mothers who can support a healthy independence in their children, but this is likely to depend on her having both internal and external support and secure adult friendships she can call on for some babysitting. Sadly, lone mothers and grand-mothers are finding the raising of boys increasingly difficult today. Yes, we do hear stories of supermums fighting the odds and sending their sons to University, while standing on their heads and saving the world, all in an afternoon.

Two problems arise from the over feminised raising of African Carib-bean boys. The first is that with the onset of adolescence there is no male role model to lock down the destructive instincts that exist within all males. Second, in his own mind no child is without a father. In the absence of a given story he will make up his own. This will usually be found among 'dons', male peer groups (who also don't have fathers).

With no contact from his father, a boy may learn from his mother only that his father is a bad man – alongside all the other men out there. A boy may even come to feel that he has descended from someone who not only could not stay at home to care for him but who would not, and therefore does not love him. Though not necessarily wholly true, this is still painful and disturbing to a child's self esteem, as much for a girl as for a boy. If the mother says good things about the absent father, that when they were together there were some good times, and that father loved his baby or his partner, or both, then the child has the chance of holding a good father in his mind. This requires brave and active mental work on the mother's part. She may despise the man or feel nothing for him, but it is possible for her to make sense of her broken relationship with the father. A bad father can still be understood, and not just re-jected out of hand. The same applies to missing mothers.

These are therapeutic tasks (Dowling and Gorell Barnes, 2000) although some fathers may be more helpful out of the picture (Jaffee *et al*, 2003) and sometimes there is very little good to tell.

The triangular predicament for boys is not unique but there are developmental differences between the sexes that make boys more vulnerable than girls to both biological and emotional stress in the early years. Because of this fragility (Kraemer, 2000) boys take up most of the time of child mental health services, while girls predominate in adolescent clinics. Whatever the underlying problem – such as an inborn tendency towards anxiety, restlessness, inattentiveness, clumsiness, learning difficulties, social aloofness, or depression – the quality of triangular relationships has a powerful influence on the outcome. Clinically, a case can be made for the familiar hypothesis that many younger boys with emotional and behavioural difficulties have powerfully enmeshed relationships with their mothers, from which the father is to some extent excluded.

For too long we have neglected to look at the impact on African Caribbean boys of having an absent father. We have been told that the black family is off limits. It has left us bereft of any meaningful studies on this topic in the UK. Before we call for change in men we will need to understand why we have resisted and hung on so doggedly for this long. This has to do with the fact that boys cannot become men without relinquishing their identification with their mothers (Greenson, 1968, Hudson and Jacot, 1991). The importance of this evidence is not diminished by the fact that many of the women seen by African Caribbean children now leave the house and go to work. This only increases the range of things women can be seen to be doing: looking after you, feeding you, doing household tasks, but also going out and coming back. Both boys and girls witness this, but the boy does not see much of the men. Many of the mothers on Generating Genius UK and Jamaica recognised this fact and wanted to send their sons to a programme that was an alternative to home. They did not just want any male; they wanted men with a caring perspective but who were unafraid to draw the lawlines.

Risk-taking

There was always a tension in my role as father-figure during the pro-gramme. To what extent was I reinforcing traditional roles and nurtur-ing these boys into becoming the isolated males that we all dislike? I had to teach these young men how to hunt: their ancestors would not forgive me if I didn't fulfill this duty. I found this to be the most fulfilling role as father-figure. The boys didn't go hunting but the programme simulated many of the elements of the hunt. The aspects of chance and personal skill are prominent in the African hunt for food and it's not sur-prising that Domino is such a popular game in the Caribbean. Players are not completely at the mercy of fate: personal skill is required. Like a hunter hoping to track his prey, the chance element is in the hand that one draws from random pieces. Thereafter the game depends on the combined skills of 'reading' – that is the ability to work out what the others have in their hand on the basis of remembering what pieces they have played up to that stage – and coordination with one's partner to outplay the opponent. According to Chevannes:

> Domino, therefore, involves both strategy and chance. It is played with a great deal of loud verbal expressions, including a liberal flow of bad words and physical gestures, which make the game characteristically male, and is usually watched by a coterie of friends. Domino is intensely popular through-out the Caribbean. (2001:162)

Let us try to imagine a hunting party in ancient times. In the simplest sense we are out for treasure, to increase our subsistence; and as the pack moves out to stalk the quarry we may see fear and anxiety in the hunters' eyes. To subdue the body that opposes us, we put aside dis-guise. We must become greater, raise the blood pressure, release the violence and resolve into one body. Our war-whoops both advertise and establish the flow of spiritual energy that binds us together. The point is that hunting does not just arise from the need for food but, like dance, also from play. The blood we raise and risk is mingled with that of our prey, whom we seem to be courting in a dance of death. By being carried into a dangerous zone of risk and unpredictability, and by offer-ing ourselves to the Luck of the day, we may rightfully take possession of this foreign body, and make it part of ourselves. Moreover if we succeed, it is not we ourselves that have prevailed but Luck, which we will learn to call the bounty of the gods. The animals we catch are both the spoils of war and a gift to the gods as well as spiritual well being.

The Generating Genius experience hopefully has left the legacy of the hunt, as handed down by the father-figure. The first activity the boys in the UK had to undertake was to develop, in groups, the best approach to tackling malaria. This was a hunt in packs, to capture the right approach to win this challenge. The boys were hungry and, at only 12 years old, they produced work that was easily at University level.

The danger with this hunting stuff is that we produce all these performance males. These are men who are great in the Lab but do no housework. As boys reject the female without, he also rejects the female within, yet this was his only hope of restraining brutal forces. It is also where he makes the decision to reject his intellect in exchange for his body. The more dangerous element in this cycle is that he despises the female that he sees in another male. What we need to teach our boys is that the hunt is really the analogy of the chase for love.

In search of a father's love

Talking to college students who are at or *en route* to University can offer insight into how they manage to navigate the challenges at school and especially the challenges facing them at home. Matthew lives with his mother and has a younger brother aged 14 and a sister of 21 who is at University. Born in Britain to Nigerian parents, he was asked to provide us with an open account of his academic success and of the biggest challenges he felt he has had to face:

> *What are your aims and ambitions over the next few years?*
> Hope to finish college and go to a good university. I hope to get straight As in my A levels. And hopefully do a placement at a hospital, shadowing doctors so I can incorporate that in my personal statement and it will help me get to Uni.
>
> *What are you studying here?*
> Biology, Chemistry, Sociology and R.E.
>
> *What is your long-term goal? What occupation do you want to follow?*
> I want to do medicine to become a doctor.
>
> *Would you regard yourself as a good student?*

I would regard myself as a good student because I've had some ups and downs but ever since I've come back from a break, where I had home problems, I enjoy my lessons. I don't give trouble to my teachers.

Secondary school: what was your relationship with your studies then?
Secondary school was pretty much the same as first year, except for my grades. I used to get into trouble a bit but my grades never dropped, they always stayed the same.

Why do you think that is, Matthew?
I don't know; when you're used to something for five years you just think if I just keep doing this, this, this and I'll keep getting this, this, this grades.

Back to college now. Do you think there is more that college could be doing to help you achieve your potential?
College has always done workshops, workshops all the time, so they cannot actually do more unless they physically come to your house and fill your head with books. So I reckon college gave me a second chance because I really messed up in first year and my grades weren't good and my A levels weren't good and they could have chucked me out but ... because of stuff going on at home, they gave me a second chance Like ... last year, apart from what I was doing in class, stuff at home was affecting me as well but I didn't tell anyone about it, I just kept it to myself But then after the first time, they started to help me more.

And how did they find out?
Because I think my mum had to tell I always thought college life and home life seemed to be completely different, should be kept separate, but then my mum came in and the college found out about her stroke. So when they found out about her stroke. Sometimes I used to say I was sick but I was actually going home to look after her.

Why didn't you tell the college that you were going home to look after your mum?
I just thought it was like begging for attention and stuff like that. I didn't want no special attention for my mum's sake like ... it's like it's my family I don't really want to get it involved with the college.

So was it an element of pride or was it personal business?
Probably a bit of both, it's still my personal business. OK ... that's college, I go to college it's different, completely different; at home that's my family. But then they could see I was struggling; I didn't want to have to admit to myself that I was struggling to try to help my mum and to also revise and keep my old social life kind of balancing it, it kind of fell apart.

With a stroke there's no warning is there? So how did it impact on you?
When it first happened it was a bit of a shock because she had never had any kind of heart problems, and no-one in my family had any type ... although my granddad did die young, but that was a special case. It just came. I'd always heard of other people having a stroke but I didn't think my mum would have a stroke. But the person who was looking after me would probably get it ... Like after my dad left she was the one to get the stroke and she did suffer, so it was a bit serious. First she lost mobility on her left side so she couldn't do too much, she couldn't really cook, she couldn't really move about the house. So sometimes I'd be late because I'd be making stuff for her to eat before I would leave for college. I'd come home and she would say she has hurt herself or something ... because she's at home and there's no-one to talk to and she's used to going to work and so she's feeling kind of down and so I'd think I need to look after her, I'll stay with her and cheer her up or something. That's what I normally do. Everyone who knows me now knows that's my personality, I'm always smiling, never frowning. I walk around the college smiling. For me to be upset takes a lot. The more I started to do that, the less I paid attention to my books so eventually my grades started dropping. I just thought 'I'll do it later'

And your mum has been the one who has been pushing your academic progress. Obviously, Dad left
My mum always emphasised education ... in primary school, in secondary school she always bought me new text books. If I broke my calculator she would buy me a new one. She wanted us to do well because she didn't finish her education until later on, she had to go back and finish it later on.

But she had a university education?
Yeah.

Has it changed your attitude to the role of women and the role of mothers in families?
Yeah, definitely, I never realised how hard she had it, but now I realise that women actually do a lot. People say men do that and men do this but women actually do a lot, like look after the kids ... Because my mum took over the dad and mum role she had extra work to do. I realised that she did a lot and it made me gain more respect for her, for what she does. It makes me want to appreciate her more.

Have you any other male role models? Anyone older than yourself in your family: uncle, grandfather, older cousin? Anyone living around you?
No not really. I see the occasional uncle but because of what my dad did it just put me off any person older than me who is a male? It's like ... don't talk

to me about my dad. I respect aunties more than I respect uncles ... I respect women more than I do men, because of that.

What was your relationship with him before he left?
I was kind of seen as my dad's favourite. Obviously no parent should have a favourite but everyone knew that I was his favourite. He was violent.

Ah, right. A very violent person. Whenever he used to come he used to hit my mum, my sister and my brother, hit me. He was very rough. He was there but he didn't really make a difference.

So he didn't help much with the chores or the responsibilities in the home?
No.

What would trigger these violent outbursts?
He used to drink quite a bit and I don't want to say anything inappropriate but he was cheap, a very cheap person. Say if we had a school trip, and we needed money for the school trip, he wouldn't give us it. And when we'd argue and ask why, he would get violent. Or something else like there'd be a letter or a bill.

He would go out and come back, he drank everything. We would confront him about his drinking and he would hit. So stuff like that.

So you don't have much contact since?
No, I've never seen or heard from him since I was about year 9.

What do you think you missed out on most, if he could have reformed his character? How do you think you could have benefited from a father's presence?
Obviously the mum can only do so much. The dad needs to be there for emotional support. You need someone who is the role, the male you want to copy like. The person you're meant to look at. I have no-one I'm meant to be looking at; my little brother is looking at me and sees: OK that's what I'm meant to do, that's the way I'm meant to act. But I only have a sister and mum. So obviously there's no-one I can look up to ... obviously I can look up to my sister but you need a male's presence, a male to teach you right from wrong. Some things that I might feel uncomfortable talking to my mum about, he can just talk to you about easily. Yeah the stronger hand. Like the mum is always there saying 'don't shout anymore' or whatever and dad is the strong 'put it down'. Yeah I would have preferred if he could have changed himself, I might have been a different person, you never *know*.

Through this project we are trying to get to the roots of why sometimes boys are left to grow up without the father's presence, not in all cases, but it does happen quite a lot. What do you think should be done? Say, with your father

and his group of men friends. Were they of a particular group? Did they be-
long to the same church? Are they of the same ethnic group? What could
have been done to get them to change their behaviour? Anything?

I really have no clue what anyone could have done, to be honest. Like there's
nothing that you could do. It's something that's always going to happen. Obviously you could say I'm going to put this limit on, but at the end of the day
it's all going to happen anyway. Nowadays it's more common to see someone
who has one parent. It's unlikely to see someone with two parents. Like, it's
more common to say 'who do you live with, your mum or your dad?' You don't
say your mum your dad; you say your mum. Nine times out of ten it's 'I live
with my mum'. It's always going to be that way. I don't know what you can do
to stop it. In some way it does actually help me because it makes me see that
I don't want to be like that. I want to grow up and look after my family, as well
as my mum. I will look after everyone because he didn't care about anyone.
My mum used to beg him to talk to his mum. All he cared about was going
out, doing whatever he wanted. People said they saw him with another
woman, stuff like that. It's just something that's always going to happen ... it
won't change anytime soon because it's not just something that's happened
to me, it happens to a lot of people.

This interview shows that our predecessors in antiracism research have
been too busy arm wrestling with notions of institutional racism. They
forgot to look at the deep emotional needs of black boys.

For Matthew, genius or success is won or lost at home. His powers of
resilience are remarkable, for he uses the hardship of the Cane Piece to
inspire him to academic progress. Nowhere in the interview does he
speak of institutional pressure, in fact college is a respite from the problems he has to face on the home front.

He applies many of the identified skills in succeeding at college, the key
one being how he chooses his friends and peers. They are clearly people
who will support his academic ambition and also give him some emotional help when he needs it.

It is when he comes to talking about fatherhood and masculinity that he
becomes most despondent. It is clear that we have a generation of black
boys who distrust their fathers and the notion of fatherhood. The hope-
ful message from the interview is that he wants for himself a redefined
notion of masculinity, which is based on being caring and taking responsibility. We must keep sight of that.

3

Finding the female within

The Blackman is to the white man what woman is to man in general, a loving being of pleasure. *F. Pruner, French Craniologist, 1868*

No woman no cry. *Bob Marley*

And the Lord said unto Cain, Where is Abel thy brother?
And he said, I know not: am I my brother's keeper? *Genesis 4 v9*

Crude thinking on gender is unhelpful. Binary lists are made of masculine and feminine attributes and the fact, as Jung reminds us, that the male has his feminine side and the female her masculine is simply forgotten.

We should speak not of masculine and feminine, but of yang and yin or Ausar-Auset – the ancient Chinese and Egyptian terms that gather and conjoin the big divide. The Chinese terms both cancel and preserve the gendering tendency, and remind us that there is no yin without yang, and that an excess of one always calls for redress from the other. Even through our most patriarchal past, males were compelled to acknowledge the central place of the feminine. Temples were built to house the yin-feminine mysteries. This yin centre was originally colonised by females and was both desired and resisted by the male. The male's problem was that even though he had instincts to hunt and fight, he was also susceptible to falling in love, this reminding him of his childhood, and hence his vulnerability. Although male and female are present within both sexes, boys are left in a restless mode. And the theatre of love constitutes a threat to male power (as all the world's mythologies testify) and one should never forget the importance of man's strong right arm in defending his interests.

The equality of having both male and female within us has left our little boys with a legacy. There is a restlessness that sees the feminine temple as a prison. I have seen this dilemma playing itself out in the lives of black boys. As a teacher, I repeatedly saw the talented black boy who can't make his mind up whether to act out a machismo caricature of himself or show the world he enjoys being school-smart.

Our fatherless homes have become a female temple which our boys want to smash during their adolescence. This is often unsafe and in-evitably self-destructive. Surely the task of civil society is to give our boys a re-taste of the feminine, an echo of his nurturing experience at his mother's breast? This can be achieved by clothing and transforming his infantile desires through art, religion and science, so that such desires can be safely housed.

This is a task for the educators and cultural practitioners working with young people. Cynics would say that it is a tough enterprise. Well, grow-ing up was always going to be tough. The case study chapters which follow reveal how, through the enterprise of Science and Engineering, our project gave the boys access to worship at the female temple within.

First we go to Jamaica, to see how the resistance to the feminine has left males marginalised and the society on the brink of anarchy. These are lessons for everyone.

The Gyalification of Man

The term 'Gyalification' was coined by Jamaican historian Clinton Hutton. In Jamaican parlance Gyal is a young woman (usually un-married) or a female child (gyal pikni). However, the term has powerful new resonance when applied in a conflict between men over status. According to Hutton (2008):

> But gyal is also used pejoratively by men in conflict to construct an effe-minate/emasculated male complex in the belligerent patriarchal culture, social psychology and ideology of Jamaica. It is this definition and use of gyal that is the focus of this essay. In the gyalification complex, a variety of sym-bolic castrations is ritualistically performed by men on men in conflict, the purpose being to 'gyalificate' or turns their opponents into women (or mama-man dem or mampaala dem).

Hutton roots much of this female phobia in the gender relations of European slavery and the subsequent colonialism and racism. There is a link with the way in which European men subjected European women: they were seen not just as second class citizens but also as powerless. Thus, white males would also maintain their supremacy over black males by 'making them girls'. Ironically, for this power-play to work, black men would also have to buy into the notion that all 'things female' was virtually death.

The enslavement of Africans effectively removed from the black male the means to provide for his family. It removed from him the basis to work harder than the black woman for their joint subsistence and consequently that core identity of manhood validated in Euro-patriarchal thought. African men were thus feminised and, like women, were deprived of the means of providing for their dearest. Black women were placed in the same predicament as black men. They too were feminised, deprived of the means of providing for their family. At the same time, black women were also masculinised, made to work just as hard as black men in order to create the value which the slaveholders always expropriated.

This politics and culture of femininity also found expression in the actions of planters who punished enslaved black men by forcing them to wear female clothes. The many castrations that White men performed on Black men during and after slavery have been well documented (Ginzburg, 1988; Hart, 2002; Hodes, 1997; Jordan, 1974). This highly feminal political act was carried out wherever black men were held in subjection by white men across the Americas. It was in the United States however, that this act became a special form of feminal institution. The purpose of castration was not just to deprive Black men *of the pleasures which they could indulge in without expense*, as James contends (1989:12). Castrating African men was the most direct way in which white men symbolically turned black men into women, into a non-political entity, into nothingness. In this way, black men would be prevented from assuming equality with white men by having sexual intercourse with white women and thus imperilling white supremacy by miscegenation.

In this state of white masculinity, extinction of Black manhood need not be performed on all Black men primarily because they needed their labour. However, men like Robert Shufeldt, the scientist and naturalist born in 1850 who once headed the Army Medical Museum in the USA, would gladly have gone all the way had it been feasible. He is on record as saying:

> It would doubtless be a capital thing, if it could be done, to emasculate the entire Negro race and all of its descendents in this country and effectually stop the breed right now and thus prevent any further dangers from them and the horrors of the crossing continuously with the Anglo-Saxon stock ... (quoted in Rogers, 1972:27).

The more white men demanded and procured sex from black women, the more enslaved black women became, as white men's sex slaves or the terrain upon which all the sexual fantasies of their imagination could be tested. Further, these men could not rid their own minds of what was an obsession with the imagined sexual prowess of black men.

By castrating/lynching the black male, the White male metaphorically captured for his own use, or destroyed for his own security, what he considered to be the essence of black manhood, of black power. By this act, the European reassured, affirmed and renewed his own manhood, his own sense of self. Trudier Harris's insight into this process is worth reading:

> For the white males ... there is a symbolic transfer of sexual power at the point of the executions. The black man is stripped of his powers, but the very act of stripping brings symbolic power to the white man. His actions suggest that, subconsciously, he craves the very thing he is forced to destroy. Yet he destroys it as an indication of the political (sexual) power he has (quoted by Wiegman in Fout and Tantillo, 1993:242).

In post-bellum America especially, a lynching can be defined as an anti-black sacrificial killing, partly driven by a frenzied coital fetishism in which the black male body is orgiastically consumed in the continuing renewal of White masculinity. An African American newspaper, The *Baltimore Afro-American* called lynching 'a type of Dixie sex perversion' (March 16, 1935). This 'sex perversion' can best be defined and described as a peculiar kind of violent homoerotic political conquest and subjection in which the conquistador assumed the role of an active homosexual and the victim an enforced homosexual passive (i.e. a kind of woman). In this campaign to emasculate black manhood so as to protect and ensure the constant renewal of white masculinity, the inescapable logic of white supremacy compels the white man to become political homosexual actives or homoerotic conquistadors. He becomes then the ultimate masculine being who is characterised by that saying or aphorism expressed among Jamaican men: '*If any hud a push a mii a push i.*' That is to say, the real masculine man will be the active partner, or the one who will be doing the penetrating.

It is this man who penetrates, and the male who is penetrated is seen as the woman or gyal. In the honorific culture which is taking root in Jamaican criminal gangs, it is said that in the construction and maintenance of status and hierarchy, subordinates or foot soldiers are known to have performed fellatio on their superiors.

Violence against or towards a perceived 'feminised male' also pervades much of youth culture in the UK. The ten year old boy Damilola Taylor was a victim of taunts of this nature. He was repeatedly ridiculed at school by being called 'gay', before he was killed in a knife attack in November 2000. Damilola's father said that his son, who had arrived in London from Nigeria only two months earlier, had no idea what 'gay' meant and during one of their long-distance phone calls, had asked his father to explain its meaning. Damilola committed the classroom crime of being different – he was Nigerian, a studious pupil, and being the new boy in class was enough for him to become a victim of name calling, including being labelled as gay. It is this equating studious with being 'non-male' that continues to haunt small black boys through their journey of adolescence. It cannot therefore be dismissed as a boyish anxiety that will be healed by the hands of time.

Gay activist Peter Tatchell observed that, 'At the time of the killing Damilola's mother told *The Independent* newspaper that Damilola had been the victim of an assault a few days before the fatal attack. His assailants accused him of being 'gay'. Other newspapers including *The Guardian* and *The Telegraph*, as well as BBC News reported the homophobic bullying and taunts of 'gay boy' directed at Damilola. Gyalification of males has not only stymied academic progress but has led to deaths.

Carolyn Cooper, a Professor of literary and cultural studies, wrote an article in the *Jamaican Gleaner* (November 2 2008) headed, 'Young men afraid to 'succeed". She speaks of how in Jamaica the use of language underpins a frightening insecurity around matters female/homosexual:

> Young men in Jamaica these days are under a lot of pressure to be straight, sexually speaking, that is. Any hint of a leaning towards homosexuality will bring down immediate judgement on their heads. So they are running scared. Even more alarming, any use of language that could even vaguely suggest homosexuality must be deleted from their vocabulary. Perfectly respectable words have taken on new meanings and now signify sexual scandal.

Professor Cooper illustrates this wonderfully with the word 'Pilot'. She asks readers to imagine a group of Jamaican pilots talking to a class of Jamaican boys about how they can succeed in becoming pilots. She goes on to say,

> So why don't our young men want to be pilots? A pilot works in a cockpit. No self-respecting Jamaican men – young or old – would admit to wanting to work there, especially bearing in mind the colloquial meaning of work as sexual intercourse. Worky-worky. (Cooper, 2008:G11)

The homo-erotic connotations given to the word 'cockpit can be left to one's imagination. We can also link cockpit to being 'female', a resting place or station for the penis. For some males, certain words are somewhat like vulgar magical spells that are pronounced onto a neutral object. Therefore a pilot in a cockpit is for many young men not an appealing image.

A similar logic is applied to the word 'succeed', which ironically has a negative meaning because of its link to the Jamaican phrase to 'Suck seed' – to suck a man's penis. Cooper also makes a link between this fear to 'succeed' and education:

> The rejection of the word 'succeed' is particularly unsettling given the fact that many young men are not succeeding academically these days. Young women are outperforming young men in high school and at university. So if the very notion of succeeding is now tainted by negative sexual allusion, how are we going to motivate young men to move past their fears and claim power? (Cooper, 2008:G11)

In many ways we have moved away from the white man's obsession with the black phallus, to the black male's 'fear and envy' of his own and his brothers 'members'. The fear of castration, however metaphorical, exists on the level of linking academic success to being made into a woman. The journey back to the female side is a long and complex one, and for some men it will take great courage.

Brother versus brother

The story of Cain and Abel can be summarised like this: God accepts Abel's lamb offering, rejects Cain's vegetables, whereupon Cain murders his brother, and is cursed by God but sanctified by a mark to preserve him in his wanderings. Some readers of this story drift into murky waters at the outset by assuming that Cain's offering is inadequate: either he was sinning in his heart or else God is telling his people not to till the ground but to keep sheep. Sociologists may want to look to some kind of social process to explain this inequality in the family. Could it be a form of institutional racism, where Cain is overlooked in favour of his brother? This is unlikely though, since they are biologically similar – African and African Caribbean perhaps? Let us assume for the purposes of this book that this is a so called 'black on black' crime. Cain is the one without luck. As it it written in *Exodus*: 'I will be gracious to whom I will be gracious' (33.19).

Cain cannot bear it; and we can empathise with him. Living as he does in the beginning, he understandably fails to make subtle distinctions between his earthly and his heavenly father, and expects as much justice from the latter as the former. We sympathise because it sounds only too familiar: is it not true that we all find our most painful childhood memories in the experience of unique parental rejection, particularly in the favouring of a sibling?

Ah yes, comes the reply, sibling rivalry is indeed a serious matter, but is it grounds for murder? Like sacrifice, murder can be best understood as the attempt to retrieve some part of one self intolerably stolen, and that the appropriate gesture for such reclamation is a bear hug that eliminates the space that separates the parties. It is here that murder and sex become two sides of the same coin. If Cain opens the door to such proffered intimacy, he shall become swollen with a power that shall at least appear to do his bidding when he 'rises up' (horny for the other) against his brother.

Engorged by the snake, Cain yearns for the ground, to ground his brother in the ground they came from, to cancel God's mistaken rejection by becoming his brother in an embrace that will eliminate forever the space between them. Whether or not one imagines a fumbling toward buggery and cannibalism here, the fumbling is important: this being the first murder, Cain does not know what he is doing, as is indicated when he says truthfully: 'I know not [where he is]: am I my brother's keeper?' The irony here is that having consumed his brother, this is precisely what he has become.

As I write, the black community in Britain faces an unprecedented level of male violence, much of it executed by the knife. Ninety per cent of these crimes are a kind of fratricide, as black youth kill each other. What is clear is the immensity of the mystery that surrounds these crimes. No one can say how they started and no one has yet come up with any answers. The Cain and Abel story gives us many clues in the search for reasons and solutions. As Charles Darwin said: 'War does not arise with scarcity ... it is instinctual'.

The British Crime Survey shows that knife and gun crime has decreased overall in the last decade, and has dropped in the capital over the last two to three years. But this good news does not extend to teenagers, especially black boys living in London, where the figures are alarming. Black boys are disproportionately at risk compared to other social groups. The other obvious challenge facing our academically successful students is the negative perceptions (deserved or not) that dominate the media regarding the activities of young black males. Sixty per cent of the headlines of the London local newspaper, *South London Press* in 2008 had a front page featuring a black gang and violence. Given the reality of street and gang violence, as well as a tirade of negative publicity about young black males, why was it that the Generating Genius boys did not bend under these pressures, which prevailed in their local communities? Why did they resist the peer pressure to turn on their brother in a fit of rage? Why were they not another statistic of school exclusion?

The answers to these questions are important not just for black males but to support the needs of all students. I found that teachers and pupils were agreed that a negative perception of black youth existed within the media and probably in the wider community. But most of our boys felt that their greatest barrier to academic success was the psychological peer group pressure from black boys in their schools and neighbourhoods who were not in the Generating Genius programme. And as I have noted, I found no evidence that black boys suffered racism, whether direct or indirect, that damaged their self esteem.

All the boys, regardless of their personality, expressed concern and anxiety about gangs, groups, and peer pressure (although there was no agreed definition of what this pressure consisted of). There was a sense that all black boys were at particular risk whether they were aware of it or not. Some had to make decisions about moving away from gangs – often a slow process. Not all had been part of a gang, although nearly all had been attacked or witnessed violence. The boys reflected on a range of strategies they employed to deal with the street but, even so, they could not predict events however careful they were.

> I worry if I'm gonna do good in my exams... I worry about getting into university ... I'm worried if I'm gonna be alive the next day? I worry something might happen ... I hear about the 25th teenager to die this year; I can tell Mum and Dad worry too ... So I say hello ... and go straight home ...

> Boys have to live up to macho behaviour – there is a lot of pressure. Boys need positive role models to show them they don't need to be macho to be successful.

> If I wasn't at Generating Genius I'd be hanging around the streets ... you meet people who want power and recognition ... I didn't get a lot of pressure ... others who were more influenced get drawn in ...

> You do tokenism to show that you are one of them but you don't get fully involved ... say your friend is arrested, you'd help your friend ... You'd show you are solid ...

> I deal with it by going with my instincts ... you need to say that you are in college or that you are working so that you can pull out...

Territoriality features heavily in the lives of our boys. Most encounter territorial behaviour mainly as victims, but not exclusively so. All the boys we interviewed felt unable to cross certain territorial boundaries. Territoriality placed limits on their freedom to go to areas outside their own, especially in the evenings and at weekends. For some the fear of violence when outside their own areas was so strong that they lived under self-imposed curfew. The ability to survive such restrictions depends on what I'd call 'street intelligence' and some boys were clearly better attuned than others to these skills.

For a small number of boys territorial behaviour was still a leisure activity. Territorial affiliations are a source of friendship, respect, protection and financial gain. One student expressed his resignation about the situation: 'that's just the way it is. If it's my time to go it's my time to go'. To escape territorial behaviour, the boys used college, athletics or football commitments. Their comments are revealing:

> You can't avoid certain people ... there are places I would avoid going ... I feel a little safe in Peckham because I went to school there ... Deptford is safe ...You are safer in Lewisham than in Catford ... but generally I am at risk anywhere

> I often think I am going to a war zone or Iraq ... I can't go to a party if I don't know who he [the host] is ... Say if my friends were to say there's a party in somewhere like Brixton ... I'm not allowed to go out. My mum worries about me being stabbed or robbed.

Conforming as resistance

The Generating Genius programme revealed how some of the boys adopted a kind of elitism predicated on academic success. As one said:

> African boys are really well educated – most of the boys on the street are Jamaicans or St Lucia, they are in trouble with the police – African boys come into class and focus, Caribbean boys just mess around.

There is a kind of standoff from certain black boys that helped them consolidate their status as a high-achieving black student. Even though he is not an academic high flyer, one boy adopts some key characteristics of conformist resistance. When I asked whether he has friends in his local area, he replied: 'Yeah – most of them are on the streets. I joined the Generating Genius to stay out of trouble'.

However our African Caribbean boys with no father at home could well challenge some of the African boys who did have their fathers at home. These boys were usually from a West African background, who faced a strict and remote father. They clearly longed for a more relaxed relationship with their father. The boys described a pattern in Black African families of strict parenting and high expectations, comparing it with the dialogue and negotiation they experienced or observed in Black British/Caribbean families:

It's like being brought up in an African household, both parents of African descent. There's like a stronger ... I don't know what it is but you have to do well. Whereas with Caribbeans, obviously they want their children to do well but it's not such a strong emphasis on doing well at school or college but with Africans it is. I don't know why.

Black African friends ... they say they want to be severed from parents, can't wait to leave home. They don't like strict rules. Whereas my Mum speaks to me on a level ... I don't want to move out (laughs).

Tensions also arose because some parents are fearful about street crime and respond by being overly protective and strict. As one boy said:

Not sure how I get on. I don't really get on with them. There is a lot of conflict. Arguments over petty things – getting a job, not calling in, staying out, they don't call me – minor things but conflict wise they become too much.

To be honest, I do my own thing ... college ... go home; get on with my thing...

I don't know, it's kind of hard ... he says he worries about the street crime but I tell him if you don't put yourself in that situation and if you carry yourself in such a manner, don't associate with wrong people ... you have to have limits to how you socialise with the wrong people.

We know dodgy guys in college or in the street but you know limits ... you don't exchange certain information with them and that's it and don't say yeah ... don't get embarrassed ... do your own thing?

The strategy of becoming a group of conformists against the world, is simply a way of thinking. It makes you radical and unashamedly different from the rest. This was a survival technique that many of our boys used in the face of continuous negative peer pressure. It worked because we now gave the boys a 'Science crew' that was safe in numbers and protected them against the anarchic instincts within and without.

In line with Generating Genius's mission to get inner city black boys into university, Derek is determined to go to into higher education after he leaves school:

I am going to my school sixth form to do A-levels in biology, chemistry and maths, and I want to go to medical school at Cambridge or Imperial. I don't know what my life would have been like without Generating Genius, it would be interesting to find out ... but I guess I'll never know.

What then is the love that has no name? The song goes 'there is a thin line between love and hate'. The spate of black male youth violence in

Homoerotic violence

Britain and the on-going male violence in Jamaica best illustrate a disguised homosexuality amongst these young men. Jamaica is particularly interesting. The combination of rabid homophobia and one of the highest male homicides in the world, tells us much. Why would you be so obsessed with homosexuality if it didn't sit on your shoulder like a bird, telling you to consume the brother you once loved? The history of slavery and poverty has made Jamaican ghettoes very violent but there are poorer places that never resort to this kind of fratricide. The real reason for the runaway violence is that Jamaican males see violence as a way of rejecting the female within; they want to make the other man a woman. This was the ultimate humiliation during slavery and now they want to do this to their brothers. The irony is that the only way you can make your brother a woman is by fucking him. It is back to the old Cain and Abel wrestling match which results in murder. In Jamaica a common retort to someone who looks at you in a disrespectful way is: 'Yuh look like yuh, a guh nyam me up'. The word 'Nyam' has a double meaning in patois. It means to eat something you like when you are hungry. It also has an aggressive meaning which means to annihilate utterly.

Homoeroticism is apparent in certain actions of the gangsters of Italy and Jamaica. Celebrated Don and gang leader Donald 'Zeeks' Phipps was convicted in 2006 for a double murder. Interestingly, the autopsy showed that Phipps's semen was inside the mouths of the two victims, revealing that before their deaths, both men had to perform oral sex on Zeeks – a final act of humiliation. This provides ritual insight into what is meant by homophobic in Jamaica. One of the most ruthless gunmen in Jamaica wants to kill the manhood inside his enemy by having them give him pleasure. It is a graphic example of sex and death in the same act.

The gangster has a number of choices once he has captured his brother: he must make him a woman, he must eat him, must wrestle with him and do whatever he needs to reincorporate him. One reason why Jamaica is so violent is that the metaphors are not wide enough to cloak the dark secrets. Wrestling and to a certain extent boxing have been a traditional metaphor to keep the destructive instincts hidden. In a matriarchal society, young men will need to invent some sacred rituals to avoid killing each other. Men have to learn ways of being intimate outside the rituals of belonging to a gang.

Cultural critics like Carolyn Cooper (2008) have argued that 'Dancehall culture' is really a big metaphor that subverts middle-class hypocrisy and double standards. She argues that gun lyrics are not the cause of violence; rather, it is a playful way for oppressed black people to be able to shoot down those who regularly disrespect them.

Jamaica's intense homophobia is also explained in such a context. I agree with Hope's (2004) 'femiphobia' thesis that the construction of the female body is a key part of how Dancehall defines its concepts of masculinity. They are inter-related. This is synonymous with Dancehall's own brand/definition of the Jamaican 'nation' wherein 'femaleness' is considered a dangerous 'state of affairs'.

Accordingly, the 'punaany' (vagina) has to be conquered as a demonstrable way of mastering sex and sexual knowledge and power in the wider society. Songs such as Shabba Ranks' *Dem Bow* makes this clear. The Jamaican 'rude boy'/'ghetto yute' is warned against performing the emasculating rituals of oral sex (with women), which gives away his (masculine) powers to this dangerous female (state). Notably, Ranks is silent on his feelings about male to male oral sex in such a context, though this is in part understood by his consistently anti-homosexual stance.

In Hope's view, Jamaican men, particularly those represented in and by Dancehall's political rhetoric/ideology, are especially concerned with emasculation. At the same time however, there are also acknowledged areas of ambivalence within these constructions, for Dancehall also re-creates elements of the homogeneity and hetero-sexism that it critiques in middle class politics within its own discourse.

Masculinity, as Cooper acknowledges, is constructed in a discourse of violence, with the male genitalia foregrounded as a central tool in the organisation of a revolutionary inner-city inspired flavour, articulated in Dancehall as political consciousness.

Hope's notion of 'femiphobia' is particularly useful, relating as it does to the central thesis of this chapter. Adolescent boys are trying to strip down their feminine side, desperately running away from the claustrophobia of their female surroundings. I am connecting two ideas here: femiphobia and violence. Once you do this simple equation, it is clear how male violence is intimately linked to homosexuality.

During the time I was researching for this book, Britain endured an out-break of knife crime violence. Young black males are killing each other. Single black mothers confessed that they fear for their teenage boys when they go out at night. At one time they would have feared racist attacks; now the greatest danger comes from young black men them-selves. What black mothers are aware of is an underlying disaffection, which they see in the day to day behaviour of their sons. In some ways the bigger violence makes the headlines – but are not bad table man-ners also important, especially if we're talking about the slippery slope into a human lunch?

I am suggesting that in our modern society, much of the stereotyping around black males is not necessarily perpetuated by white main-stream society but rather by the black males themselves. Of course there are expectations about big black men that run through the current of mainstream society in both the UK and the Caribbean. We do however need to understand the power of black on black expectation, to see its implications for education and even for survival on the street. We have been so obsessed with what white people think and do to black people that we've not understood the impact we have on each other. Some would argue that this doesn't matter, because the real elephant in the room is the white person and white institutional racism. This book argues that, like those God-is-dead theories, the white man is not the big barrier to a good life. It is In fact the ghost of the white man which is conjured, mainly by certain white researchers and black activists who have a vested interest in keeping him alive. If that is the case then those who are haunted by the ghost of the white man are those we need to fear and to help them to exorcise that ghost.

This discussion seeks to shine a light out of the darkness and help return us to 'intimacy'. We need to find a way back to the feminine in our culture that has linked it with oppression and repression. Again, Jamaica has given us some light in the darkness. It has had a healthy tradition of males singing love songs, about men being fulfilled when they re-connect with their lost beloved. The songs speak of broken hearts. Many are Jamaicanised versions of American RnB records but a love song tradition does exist. I am not expecting Jamaican male singers to start singing love songs to their male friends but they do have to open up their 'female side' in order to make these tunes.

The other creative space where you can safely become 'feminine' is to use your intellect. Professor Rex Nettleford, former Vice-Chancellor of the University of the West Indies says he tells his male students to worship the head that comes out of the shirt-collar rather than the one that emerges from the pants zipper.

Acting white

The way black males in the Diaspora position each other has become a powerful force. Those who engage in intellectual activity, like speaking in 'standard English' and achieving well academically, are often viewed with suspicion. That is, in the UK and US, they may be labelled as 'sell-outs' to the white establishment, whereas in Jamaica the perception of them extends to labels of middle-class or feminine. There is again a sexualisation and racialisation of those who conform to mainstream schooling and do well within the system.

The idea that students are powerless victims in a wider 'game' of institutional racism is nothing less than patronising. Even when faced with white racism, these black students are their own worst enemies. According to black Berkley scholar John Mcwhorter (2000):

> The 'acting white' charge – which implies that you think yourself different from, and better than, your peers-are the prime reason that blacks do poorly in school. The gifted black student quickly faces a choice between peer group acceptance and intellectual achievement. Most, out of an utterly human impulse, choose the former. Even if they open themselves to schooling in college or later, their performance all too often permanently suffers from the message they long ago internalised that 'the school thing' is an add-on, not a mix-in. (2000 p45)

The cult of anti-intellectualism pervades black American culture, and according to scholars Signithia Fordham and John Ogbu (1986), is the main reason for underachievement:

> One major reason black students do poorly is that they experience inordinate ambivalence and affective dissonance in regard to academic effort and success. This problem arose partly because white Americans traditionally refused to acknowledge that black Americans are capable of intellectual achievement and partly because black Americans subsequently began to doubt their own intellectual ability, began to define academic success as white people's prerogative, and began to discourage their peers, perhaps un-

consciously, from emulating white people in academic striving i.e. from 'acting white.' (Fordham and Ogbu, 1986)

We need to think about re-working the definition of 'institutional racism' and we need to talk about how black students begin 'to discourage' their peers. The idea that black underachievement is the result of 'unwitting' racism by teachers may have been true in the distant past. However, good qualitative research in the UK as well as in the US reveals that the biggest barrier to educational attainment facing black boys is actually black peer pressure.

The journey to find the female within in a female-phobic context is never going to be easy. Just as cats find it easier to climb up a tree than to come back down, it is easier on the mind to undertake a war than to come back home. Hence the instincts of our boys can work in wartime but need to be tamed for civil society and fulfilment of their own potential. We have shown that just as the white man has become obsessed with the black phallus, the black male has failed to take advantage of the post-civil rights freedoms because he has been too obsessed with the white man's phallus. If he really wants to be free he needs to find the female within. One that comprises of a new masculinity and not one made up an African version of a European masculinity. He needs to literally get his teeth out of white maleness and take the tough journey home. He will require help though, as he faces some big monsters and many distractions. Institutional racism may well exist but the nastier demons are lodged within.

Parents ... too little breast milk

Data from the 2007 UNICEF report on Gender disparities in Jamaica looks specifically at the gender-based vulnerabilities to HIV, early pregnancy and violence. The report shows that close to half of Jamaican households (46.3%) are headed by women. In the poorest areas, the proportion increases to 54 per cent. Resources available to children in female headed households are therefore scarcer than for children living in male headed households.

In more than 78 per cent of cases, female headed homes are actually single-woman headed households, which means that children living in 36 per cent of the Jamaican households grow up without an adult male figure. Many men are absent because they are in prison, died a violent death, or simply because they do not care. Quite often the boys grow up without knowing their fathers, whose names are absent from their birth certificates.

To many children even the experience of living in a household is unknown. In December 2005, a total of 2,497 children (70% of them boys) were living in institutions – children's homes or places of safety. Even though increasing numbers of children end up in foster care, this is not the case for boys. Males end up in children's homes more often than girls and are less likely to be placed in foster care where they can grow up in a family environment.

Further, the infant mortality rate, estimated at 17 per 1,000 live births, is higher for boys than for girls. The under-five mortality rate – or probability of a child dying before his/her fifth birthday has not significantly declined in the last decade, and there is a 3-4 per cent gender gap, to the detriment of boys. According to the UNICEF report:

> This gap seems to be partly accounted for by significant gender disparities in some health care practices, right from birth, as no significant gender gap can be found in the incidence occurrence of the most common childhood diseases and conditions ... Exclusive breastfeeding best promotes proper nutrition, emotional development and a healthy start in life. Yet according to the 2005 MICS, and within a context of very low exclusive breastfeeding (15.2% of children aged 0-5 months were found to be exclusively breastfed) boys are half as likely as girls to benefit from the practice. (UNICEF, 2008)

Put simply, Jamaican mothers are less likely to breastfeed their sons – whether or not this is a pattern right across the black Diaspora needs more research What we do know is that in 2001, 69.5 per cent of women in the US (46.3% exclusively) breastfed their infants in the early postpartum period. In the same year, only 32 per cent of mothers were still breastfeeding (17.2% exclusively) at 6 months postpartum. In 2001, only 52.9 per cent of African American women breastfed their infants in the early postpartum period, compared with 73 per cent of Hispanic mothers and 72 per cent of white mothers. The proportion of African American mothers continuing to nurse 6 months after birth was only 22 per cent, compared with 3 per cent of Hispanic mothers and 34 per cent of white mothers. These rates underscore a significant racial/ethnic disparity in breastfeeding rates.

Dr. Suzette Oyeku comments on this trend in the July-August 2003 issue of *Public Health Reports*. In her article 'A Closer Look at Racial/Ethnic Disparities in Breastfeeding', Oyeku reports that of all the factors influencing a woman's decision to breastfeed, the two most critical sources of information were from healthcare providers and social supports (friends and family). Black women signing up for support during the time preceding her study were more likely to be advised to bottle-feed than their white counterparts because they were more likely to return to work sooner than non-black women and wouldn't be working in situations suitable for pumping.

Breastfeeding and later cognitive and academic outcomes

In its Health and Development Study, Horwood and Fergusson of Christchurch School of Medicine in New Zealand examined the associations between the duration of breastfeeding and childhood cognitive ability and academic achievement of children from age 8 to 18 years. From the data collected during the course of an 18-year longitudinal study of a birth cohort of 1000 New Zealand children, they concluded:

> ... that breastfeeding is associated with small but detectable increases in child cognitive ability and educational achievement. These effects are 1) pervasive, being reflected in a range of measures including standardised tests, teacher ratings, and academic outcomes in high school; and 2) relatively long-lived, extending throughout childhood into young adulthood. (Horwood and Fergusson, 1998)

The politically correct lobby has strangely avoided this kind of research, afraid that we would sink into some kind of biological pathology. Jamaica has too many male homicides to worry about such posturing. What it does point to is a gender discrimination against boys which occurs right from the time of the breast.

The origin of this type of socialisation stems from efforts by parents to toughen their boys and prepare them to fend for themselves, as they are expected to do in society later on. Even when mothers spoil their sons by allowing them to do far fewer household chores than the girls, the intention is to make them macho by their not having to do 'girly' things. But I return to the matter of the breast for it has serious implications for the journey towards manhood.

I have sub-titled this book *black boys' search for ritual and love*. One of the things love seeks is a return to our initial playful world where we first experience trust, security, and intimacy. Since that was a world we knew on one person's breast only, it makes sense to seek its retrieval under similar exclusive conditions. As infants of species are bonded to their mothers by the experience of visual, auditory or olfactory imprinting, one may imagine something similar in the case of love occurring, such as through the eyes. The eye is not only our most expressive and individual feature but the staring eyes can also mean a prelude to war or gang fights. Staring intently may even be taboo amongst some, except however, when with a mother or lover, where the eye dilates, melts and promises union. Once again we observe the close link between love and hate: no wonder so many fights in the playground begin with the words 'What are you staring at?'

Love and subsequently religion begin in the attempt to retrieve the security and delight first tasted at a mother's breast. What if, as in the proven case of Jamaican boys, the breast were withdrawn? What then are the consequences for male development? The result appears two-fold: first, immaturity, and secondly, blockages occur to accessing the female within. Boys grow up feeling deprived and emotionally undernourished.

It is not surprising that it is in the male fantasy of the gang that some boys seek to replace this gap in their nourishment with homoerotic attachment. They deliberately stare into the eyes of their rivals, wanting to provoke them, making them stiff and primed for delicious consumption. We need only listen to the narratives of Jamaica's notorious gang leaders to find a pattern. The majority never knew their fathers and were raised early on not even by their mothers but by their grandmothers. For these men the breast of their mothers was too quickly withdrawn, unlike their sisters who fed longer on the milk of human kindness.

Certain key implications for policy and parental advice arise. Much of the discussion around black boys and achievement has centred on trying and often failing to connect black father figures or role models with boys. There is no doubting the serious impact that an under-fathered community has on black boys. However, we might be able to do more if mothers understood better how to raise their sons. This would take us away from the unhelpful blame culture that surrounds single black mothers. Mothers would be educated not only to give their sons equal access to the breast but also to re-think their nurturing of them. The Jamaican UNICEF research reveals gross gender disparities when looking at the emotional and health needs of boys and girls.

In Jamaica, the choice of health provider and the amount of money spent on care seems also to be heavily influenced by gender considerations. Mothers were found to be more likely to take their boys to government hospitals (45.5% for boys and 28.7% for girls) and their girls to more costly private physicians (43.3% for girls and 15.2% for boys). The statistics on money spent on medication for children shows that considerably less is spent on boys than on girls. This means that families are spending more on the daughters' health than that of their sons', especially within the first five years of their lives.

The report also shows that more boys than girls tend to suffer from neglect and punishment. Relying on various forms of violence is commonly used to control children aged between 2 and 5, but it is used more often on boys. Amongst children aged 5 or under, it is boys more than girls that endure inadequate care, thereby being exposed to more risks or hazards such as sexual abuse.

When analysing the results of the Grade One Readiness Inventory (GRI), a tool intended to assess mastery of the skills children need in order to begin the Jamaica Grade 1 curriculum, boys were found to be twice as likely as girls to fail to master any of the subscales.

The data from the report reveals a pattern of gender disparity that is generally to the detriment of boys. It indicates that there is a need to better understand the early construction of gender roles through gender socialisation, mothers' and fathers' expectations of their children and their behaviour towards boys and girls. Early childhood specialists seem to agree that parents are paying greater attention to their daughters whom they consider to be more fragile and in need of greater protection than their sons of the same age. Conversely, the apparent neglect in boys' care seems to stem from the desire to toughen them up and prevent them turning into a 'mama man' or mummy's boy.

It isn't surprising that so many boys want violently to break up the female temple within themselves and others. The key quality that children receive on a biological as well as an emotional level is resilience.

Nurturing and underachievement

One of the urban myths that has been doing the rounds of the antiracist forums in Britain is that Black boys enter the education system at age 4 or 5 intellectually ahead of other ethnic groups and are performing the worst by the time they are 10 or 11. This myth is proof that the white man or woman has damaged the superior genius of the black boy. I have however, found little statistical evidence to support this claim. In fact there is more evidence to support the Jamaican research that points to a positive early parenting factor as opposed to a negative one that sustains development and growth.

A study of the English National Curriculum Key Stage 1 results taken when children are 7 shows black Caribbean pupils are performing poorly. To attribute this to teacher racism does not make sense. These children have clearly been influenced by parenting, culture and poor nurturing before they entered the schooling system. Look at the city of Manchester's results for all pupils based on gender:

% LEVEL 2+	2007			2008		
	BOYS	GIRLS	ALL	BOYS	GIRLS	ALL
Reading	70.7	79.7	75.1	71.8	81.3	76.6
Writing	68.6	76.8	70.1	64.1	76.9	70.5
Maths	84.1	85.3	84.7	83.2	86.8	85
Science	80.4	83.4	81.9	78.8	84.4	81.6

At the end of Key Stage 1, over half of the ethnic groups are performing in line with the Manchester average, with White British, Black African, Indian and Pakistani pupils performing well in reading, writing and maths. More than half of ethnic groups show higher performance than in 2007, notably in reading.

Chinese pupils are the only ethnic minority pupils to achieve over 90 per cent in maths, but have declined in performance in all three subjects. For the first time in six years, Chinese pupils have achieved results for reading which are below the Manchester average.

Black Caribbean pupils have also declined in performance, particularly for reading and maths, by 9.1 per cent and 8.6 per cent respectively.

Somali pupils are still performing below the Manchester average, yet have made improvements in all results, particularly in reading. Irish pupils have declined in writing by a significant 16.1 percentage points.

These early results for children indicate that what happens between the ages of 0-5 (pre-school) will determine the school outcomes for children age 7.

The endangered black goddess

I have laid out a case in which the nurturing of black boys can explain their difficulty in making that journey form boyhood to manhood. Implicit in this text could be a reading that blames black women – the major care-givers. I want to suggest that this may well be the case but in many instances, these are unintentional outcomes and can be excused. Raising boys is no easy task, especially in a world where the male ego rules supreme.

Rivalry and envy

The fact that male deities replaced female ones and took over their reproductive powers strongly suggests an attack on women driven by envy (Kraemer, 1991). Relative equality gave way to the inequality of the sexes characteristic of historic times. Men's status or prestige was increased, but at great cost to their modesty, their capacity to love. As feminist scholars such as Redfearn (1992) have shown, the political, intellectual and artistic achievements of women throughout history have been largely ignored. But because vulnerability and tenderness are projected onto women, the definition of maleness becomes rather hollow, encouraging performance at the expense of genuineness.

> It is as if the symbol of authority is a hard father who is not yet assured of loving and being loved, a narcissistically wounded or deprived person who, despairing of being loved, resorts to force and legalistic principles and reinforces this way of feeling secure by accentuating masculine-feminine polarities and subjugating females and female deities. (Redfearn, 1992:188)

Something happened to men all those years ago that is only now becoming clear. This is partly because the story of the world was written by men who could not question their superior role in it. The black male will always have ambivalence about his female side. The legacy of slavery left him thinking that to become female was to submit to the horrors of white supremacy. That's why so much Black Nationalism continues to feel so machismo and anti-female. It literally wants to throw out the female with the racist bathwater. Paul Gilroy, makes this point somewhat laboriously in his book, *Between Camps*:

> Black feminist analysis has rightly repudiated the identification of the race's fortune with the public integrity of its masculinities. The impact of its critiques has added substantially to uncertainty about collective particularity and the conditions in which racialized solidarity can emerge and be sustained. (Gilroy, 2000:213)

Generating Genius steered clear of overt black nationalism. We wanted the boys not to be obsessed with white racism but to have the confidence to resist it. To find the female within meant learning two things: how to love each other and how to love your own mind. There was no need to teach this through propaganda. We saw the importance of performance but we were not going to become black minstrels, all body and no mind.

The irony was that Generating Genius is based on an all boys programme. In the early feminists days there was a strong emphasis on women having 'a room of their own'. The idea was that you could briefly escape the toll of patriarchy and build a woman's movement, without ego driven men telling you how to run things. For black boys the same logic applies. They needed to escape from their mothers, grandmothers and female teachers, not to find the beast within but to learn how to safely become female. How to lay down their arms and join civil society. In our group discussions in the evenings, boys were able to open up and talk about the pressures of balancing the male and female. Some spoke about how their mothers suffocated them, making them feel more aggressive. Such discussions would have been highly unlikely with girls in the room.

Rites of passage

In non-modern societies the transition to adulthood not only had a formal marker but often included a particular challenge. Among the Omaha Native Americans for instance, young men would go out alone into the desert, they would fast, and return telling stories of the visions they had experienced. The elders of the village would pronounce on whether or not these visions were real and proclaim the youths' status as an adult. These seem to be sensible and caring rites of passage. However, too many rites and rituals have developed so that young men emerge denying the 'female' or in some cases abusing women.

The Generating Genius strategy was to create rites of passage that helped boys find the softer skills such as conflict management, flexibility and the great asset of self-reflection. However the real skill was taking on the pressure of a world that still could not accept a black man with brains, pressure that came not only from white society but also from black peers. Giving our students the opportunity to do summer schools in majority white Universities while at the same time exposing them to black academics helped to kill any doubts that the world was their oyster. This was not a strange initiation into black male nationalism; rather, it sought to get our boys to adopt the strategy that was working for their sisters. An ethnic breakdown of recent GCSE results in England shows that 'black African' girls are scoring higher grades than 'white British' boys. The qualities of black female success are ironic because they are very masculine, Lynda Stone in her *Education Feminist Reader* says:

> During my education my father was an active source of encouragement, offering as much support as he was able to. More importantly, given the links between the culture of the home and school may be weak, the link between the kinds of values that are fostered in black girls and those of the mainly male-oriented culture of the school are strong. It would seem that the female gender role constructed within black families displays features that are more often associated with the male gender role in British culture. Qualities such as independence, self-reliance, and a sense of responsibility for others are very much part of the essential attributes associated with black families. Research has shown that school cultures actually favour those who possess such traits, and it is the view of the writer that this attitude operates to encourage the success of black girls in certain spheres of school life. (Stone and Bolt, 1994:235)

Like these successful black girls, the boys at Generating Genius would have to climb three hurdles to successfully complete their rites of passage:

■ the mainstream – ie white middle class culture, teachers, curriculum

- the minority experience – racism, labelling, stereotyping
- the comfort zone of conforming to peer pressure – being called a sell-out for doing well in school)

Black, mixed heritage or working class students who successfully negotiate this journey are more likely to:

- develop peer relationships across racial, ethnic, class, and gender boundaries;
- participate in popular and unusual extracurricular activities such as football and chess
- internalise only those mainstream values they define as necessary for their academic achievement
- develop coping strategies to overcome inconsistencies between mainstream (white middle class) values and their home and community values
- develop peer relationships across racial, ethnic, class, and gender boundaries;

Clifton spoke of his ability to cross racial barriers and how that made him a confident all-rounder:

> But, you know, I grew up in school being the only black student in my class. So that makes it a lot easier because a lot of the courses are European biased and a lot of Black people are scared to step out of their racial boundaries and, you know, explore other people, other cultures. So the fact that I have been raised around different races made it a lot easier.

Not all our boys played football: unusually for black boys we had one tennis champion and a young golf star. Calvin told us:

> Tennis is just a passion. I always loved sports particularly basketball, but I'm very short. So my parents got me tennis lessons when I was younger. And one of the things I appreciate about that is it's a way for me to meet different people because the basketball squad is of course all black and tennis is predominantly white, and so a lot of my white friends came from here.

For Stephen, success was about being a pragmatist – a trait often found in black girls.

> I'm not saying that all that we do in school is bad ... some of it is just necessary to pass the exams. Take this white poet Edgar Allen Poe... I don't give a

xxxx about him and his life, yet next week I've got to do a seven page essay on him. I'm into rap ... players like Biggie and Tupac.

Students who were from poor backgrounds did develop coping strategies to overcome the gulf between mainstream values and their home and community values. A boy whom I personally mentored over some years told me:

It's funny, when the acceptances from Universities started to come in I didn't say anything ... because you know some people might have felt awkward particularly if they didn't get a place. I just decided to say nothing. And when my mother asked me each morning 'Did you get any college news' ... I finally said 'Oh I got into Cambridge' She nearly strangled me. She couldn't understand why I wasn't more excited. In my neighbourhood you've just got to keep your cool if you want to stay cool and not appear better than anyone else.

Cultural wars

I suggested earlier that one way in which males can preserve the female temple within is through the arts and culture. We sing love songs and dance so that we can house those female sensibilities and make ourselves social beings. Imagine for a minute the soul and reggae love crooners Dennis Brown, Otis Redding, Al Green and Alton Ellis singing not about real women but to the female within another man or themselves. I see these love songs as incantations or spells that are trying to wake up the goddess within. We need to listen again to that wonderful song by Bob Marley 'No Woman no cry'. It needs to be sung before we go to war, a lullaby to calm the instincts. Notice Marley is talking about a journey, an odyssey, in which he comforts his woman with fond memories and words of kindness. The song is also about the existential Rastafarian travelling alone who finds comfort and redemption from the woman within:

I remember when we used to sit
In the government yard in trench town.
And then georgie would make the fire lights,
As it was logwood burnin through the nights.
Then we would cook cornmeal porridge,
Of which I'll share with you;
My feet is my only carriage,

So I've got to push on through.
But while I'm gone:

No, woman, no cry;
No, woman, no cry.
Woman, little darlin, say don't shed no tears;
No, woman, no cry.

It is interesting that popular Jamaican male musicians have become less interested in wooing women and more interested in reflecting the arm-wrestling/gun culture of the ghetto. Yet when a love song does break out it is extremely popular, especially amongst the female audience. Black male music culture over the last 25 years has seen a struggle between the rebellious hyper-masculinity of some rap music and its longer tradition of love songs. I have no doubt that the less we sing to our female soul the more disinterested she becomes – and one day she packs her bags and leaves. Our music turns into a kind of homo-erotic orgy, calling and pulling us back to our base instincts. We can see this on the You-tube gangster rap offering made in tribute to a teenage gang member shortly after his murder.

On the positive side, black male music and dance has produced a wonderful inventiveness. Dance has also allowed us to free ourselves from what Rex Nettleford (1995) describes as 'the European puritan ethic', which condemned the expression of the body. In Black communities, it would be less inhibited working class people who would not only see dance as appropriate for men but use it to transform other forms of expression like cricket or athletics.

The body belonging to the oppressed is a powerful means of communication and for the self to have control over it places it beyond the reach of the oppressor. Cricketers and dancers who cannot express themselves well in writing can nonetheless communicate. So West Indian cricketers of the1950s and 1970s were brashly and defiantly beautiful to behold, even when they were losing! The celebration of the male body as hot-blooded power and authority in itself, as an icon of athleticism, line and form became a psychological threat to opponents in colder climes. The arrogant sensuality of striding men, the white cloth draped around their dark skins, advancing with stylish swagger towards the crease... It would be the women who would comment on not only the batting technique but the sexiness of their men in white.

The phrase 'dancing down the wicket' is favoured by journalists and broadcasters because they understand cricket and dance to experience a shared aesthetic base. 'Dancing down the wicket' actually refers to a batsman leaving his crease or area of safety to attack the bowler as if by pre-emption. The bowler/batsman encounter and the rhythms involved are reminiscent of the point/counterpoint aspect of music and dance.

The example of cricket is significant. Here is a classical English game, usually associated with older white and upper-class people. The young West Indian cricketers in the 1970s didn't break their bats and complain about institutional racism. They looked to the female within, the creative muse that would inspire them to re-invent the game on their terms.

Poet Derek Walcott has attacked those who perceive Caribbean people as having no culture. They are, he says, sadly mistaken. For him, the strength of the African Caribbean male has been in the way he tries to make his fragmented culture whole. Walcott argues that the culture is often superior to the Old World, which never appreciates the effort of remaking cultures afresh, but that the African Caribbean genius is condemned to contradict itself. To celebrate Shakespeare, cricket and Western style Christianity might be, to some, to celebrate the old plantation system. However, Walcott sees the Caribbean Diaspora as creating fresh people, fresh images and a fresh language, which emerges from the reworking of these old fragments. It can never be a mimic culture – literature, sport and religion will always be painted anew.

Walcott's ideas on creativity can be applied to the way we teach the curriculum. What seems to be missing is the 'old school' methodology which our ancestors learnt not in ancient Egypt, but in the cane field. This is never taught. Modern black genius has always been in the way old things are made new. That which was given was re-made into a luxury product available to all. The best example of this is jazz. Stanley Crouch speaks about the democratic values of jazz for America:

> In essence, then, the Constitution is a document that functions like the blues-based music of jazz: it values improvisation, the freedom to constantly re-interpret the meanings of our documents.

> These musicians hear what is played by their fellow performers, are inspired to inventions of their own, hold their places in the forms of songs and send tasks to their muscles so that all functions of mind and body come together with remarkable speed. (Crouch 1995)

Crouch is talking about how jazz is a deliberate assembly of different parts coming together to make musical sense during the act of playing. We are coming close to a method of generating genius. For me it would be getting groups of black boys together in smart suits, teaching them how to play together, giving them space to be individuals, developing leaders, encouraging originality and the use of their hands, stimulating their brains, encouraging listening skills and doing the big man thing – giving a performance. No wonder the jazz player remains the classic black sex icon.

Cultural and social capital can take numerous forms. Cheron Byfield (2008) identifies a form which enables black boys to achieve against the odds. Whilst the possession of a high degree of dominant cultural capital is widely recognised as a key contributory factor to academic achievement, the contribution of other forms of non-dominant capital is often overlooked. Byfield's qualitative study of educationally success-ful Black males in the UK and the USA, involving 40 black male students who attended both new and ancient universities, found religion to be a contributory factor to the educational success of Black male students. Their church community engineered cultural and social capital. Further, the students' belief in God engineered religious capital, all of which significantly enhanced these students' academic achievement. It is not surprising that black churches across the Diaspora have on aver-age 70 per cent female attendance. In many communities the church has become the last hope for civil society.

A man's place in the modern world

Too much of the debate about black boys takes place without any link to their emotional and psychological development. There are certain universals that seem to cross all cultures.

At some time after their second birthday boys begin to sense gender difference. This depends on being able to see the naked bodies of girls and boys, but also on the insistence of his care-takers that he is a boy, which means he is not like a girl. The girl is having complementary ex-periences, receiving the same gendering message: that she is a girl, and not a boy. The difference is that she is surrounded by women, so she can see what she is meant to become (Phillips, 1993). The importance of this evidence is not lessened by the fact that many of the women children see now leave the house and go to work. This only increases the range of things women are seen to be doing: looking after you, feeding you, doing household tasks, but also going out and coming back. Both boys and girls witness this, but the boy does not see much of the men.

Logic dictates that if the male is different, then he must be unlike the female. The only thing to do is to give up everything to do with female and set off into the darkness to become one of those mysterious and powerful absent males. This is equivalent to the rise of the creator gods at the beginning of history. In order to feel male he has to jettison what he perceives as maternal qualities by putting mother down. As Jalmert (1990) says:

> the positive outcome of this development is that the boy will see himself as separate with marked boundaries. The negative outcome is that the boy will have difficulties in getting close to other persons. We might even call it a fear of intimacy'. (p3)

This sounds like a reasonably accurate description of far too many men.

It does not have to be like that. If the man's place were like the woman's, both in the home and out of it, the boy would not have to grow up in this way. I do not mean that he will be able to avoid the negotiation of the delicate passage from dependent infant to assertive gender-conscious toddler. But with adult males around him he can see for himself what he might become, and there would at once be more variety in his experience. Nor do I mean that men have to be the same as women (the inevitable segregation of sport will see to that!), but a greater range of identities and roles can become available for them, just as they have for modern women. For a child of either sex, a *real man* is so much more interesting than an absent fantasy, whichever exciting or important things he may be doing. Notice that I say a real man, a phrase normally reserved for one with particularly impressive powers, political, muscular or sexual. The trouble with that model, as we have seen, is that it requires putting women down.

Men as role models

It should be clear enough that if we had a greater variety of relationships between men and women as parents, there would be a corresponding greater variety of gender identities. This is particularly urgent now because of the imminent extinction of the 'old man' without any plausible successor waiting in the wings ... Oh I almost forgot: we have the British government's REACH project which plans to replace absent black fathers with black upwardly mobile role models. The programme was fronted by black celebrities including top male fashion designer Ozwald Boateng. He wears the sharpest of suits, is a respected family man and one of world's greatest male designers. So why is it that I think Ozwald Boateng's role model scheme is as ridiculous as a baggy suit?

This scheme is not only fundamentally flawed but also an immense waste of Mr Boateng's abundant talent. What he should have instead been organising, is a black male version of Project Runway. Go into our communities and encourage some of our boys to 'use their hands' and their imaginations in creating new lines of male fashion. He should then run a competition which could be a cross between Project Runway and The Apprentice. The winner would have the chance to work for Mr Boateng in his flash fashion house. Now *that's* how you transform our youth and get a sense of aspiration. So we have role models and then more role models, followed by even more role models. What does this change? What have the youth really learned once you've told them how wonderful you are?

When I ask young boys both here and in the Caribbean what they really want from their elders, they answer that they want boundaries that are strict and fair, and activities that are productive and stimulating. Yes, many will drop into fantasy and say they want football fame or a million pounds now. However once the fantasy is stripped back, you find the real person and their reasonable demands.

We are at such a critical point with our youth that we can't afford to allow the unimaginative to be running the shop. The result will always be bankruptcy. The creative Mr Boateng said that: 'There is a real need to inspire young black men to achieve by demonstrating how different black men from similar backgrounds are doing well in all kinds of different positions.' We are back to 'performance'. The problem with schemes like REACH is that our boys become voyeurs, peeping at the performance of the role model, who will never be able to replace that withheld breast of the mother or those loving boundaries that were laid down by a caring father.

Yet there is a great deal of anxiety about change, because whether we like it or not it is happening now. The contortions of politicians trying to defend the old moral order are just one sign of widespread panic. This is nowhere more evident than in the threatened male and his well documented backlash. It is quite wrong to state that women's liberation has gone far enough, when it has hardly started. But the shrillness of the opposition to change must not be disregarded. What we may be witnessing is the beginning of the end of a really ancient patriarchal structure. How can this possibly happen without real fear on the part of men (and even women) everywhere, a fear which could produce further and ever more desperate efforts to reassert authority?

Either the frightened male is defeated, in which case the backlash will be all the more violent and possibly terminal, or he is taken on board as a thinking human being. For the latter to happen, he will need to be brought up differently. In spite of everything, there are many signs of change. Most men attend the delivery of their children now, compared with hardly any thirty years ago. But they still receive little social encouragement to participate as parents, even though we know that many men are now keen to do their share (Kraemer, 1994). Or at least they say they are – which is a good start. When they do, it increases the richness of the children's experience from infancy right up to adulthood (Lamb and Oppenheim, 1989, Russell and Radojevic, 1992, Pruett, 1993). But it would also make a difference to our expectations of men in general.

If the instincts of young males are geared up for war, how do we calm and deflect their desires? This problem was identified in ancient Greek myth, the Old Testament and post-independent Jamaica. They give us the stories and songs that tell us how to prevent the instincts of young males destroying the civil community and, in the process, themselves. If we have only read in the limited literature of Education Sociology we should go back to basics and re-read the stories from our childhood.

During his travels, Odysseus negotiates a compromise between travel for the sake of curiosity and applied intelligence geared to the achievement of identified goals. This tension is expressed when Odysseus meets the Sirens and finds a way to acquire both knowledge for its own sake (there is no need for him to hear their song) and to protect his own safety and his men's. The solution is technological – wax ear-stoppers and bonds attached to the mast to stop them following the Sirens' call. Here Odysseus becomes a model for scientific inventiveness, an ancient James Bond.

It seems vital to me that before our young men embark on the treacherous journey of adolescence, they avoid the mistakes of their forefathers. They will need to chart a route that is not obsessed with arm-wrestling white men. If they are to do any wrestling then it should be with each other, making sure that the bear-hug doesn't turn into a frenzied homo-erotic dinner. It would be good to give our young men the wonderful stories of Cain and Abel, folk-tales that gives civil society its structure. This will be tough in a secular society that regards the Bible as boring and the Greeks as irrelevant. It isn't surprising that the young men who live close to the church or the lessons of the ancient myths seem to be the ones who succeed in today's world.

CASE STUDIES

Generating Genius is one discrete and effective project but it is by no means the only strategy for bringing boys back to schooling. The two case studies that follow offer a broader perspective on approaches that succeed against the odds. Both are the more remarkable for being drawn from islands that are struggling with problems of masculinity and boys' achievement in often impoverished and difficult conditions. in both countries, the raising of and caring for boys has become a key feature of social policy. And both offer impressive models of good practice, telling the wider story of how boys can be helped to succeed.

Chapter 4 presents a case study of a school in Samoa. It is a secondary school, a Catholic technical centre attended by boys who have not succeeded at other schools and who need ritual, love and schooling. The results offer inspiration and guidance that can be widely applied.

This is true also of Chapter 5, the case study of a primary school in a poor part of Jamaica. The new Principal, Mrs Bolt, has turned the school around through a sustained programme, Change from Within. It illustrates how strong and directional leadership can establish lasting change for the staff, pupils and the community.

4

Learning how to serve: SAMOA

Introduction

There is no Samoa-based review or research into the under-achievement of boys or the best classroom practice for them. There is awareness of the issue though, as noted in various reports on participation, national examination results and review of the education sector. Discussions with many of the secondary school Principals regarding the achievement of boys, acknowledged awareness of and concern over boys' underachievement. However, this awareness has yet to translate to specific strategies aimed at increasing boys' achievement in regular mainstream schools.

The following case study is based in Pacific Technical, a Catholic technical centre specifically set up to focus on the development of boys within an atmosphere characterised by a sense of spiritual awareness, values of lifelong learning, leadership and service. The aim of describing the case study is to identify innovative approaches used in the school to support boys' development that are transferable to other contexts.

The case study begins with background information on the school, followed by the methodology used. It goes on to describe reported evidence of innovative approaches to the teaching and learning of boys – innovations which are identifiably different from the typical programmes within the secondary school sector and concludes with the implications for schools.

Background

Pacific Technical Centre opened in 1989 as an all-male institution that responds to the needs of marginalised boys who had left regular formal secondary schools without qualification or the skills for employment. It is part of a world wide family of institutions named for the founder of the Salesian Society, St. John Bosco or, as he is commonly called, 'Don (Father) Bosco', a 19th century Italian priest who established several technical schools to train boys to be skilled craftsmen and leaders. With the idea of empowering the most vulnerable boys, the Centre commits to the holistic development of boys through focusing on technology education, career preparation and opportunities to develop social awareness.

The Centre opened in 1989 with 32 students, and by 2005 there were 250 pupils attending the Centre. It is about ten minutes from the centre of the capital and only town, Apia. Owned by the Salesian Congregation, a religious congregation of priest and brothers founded by Pacific Technical, it has a staff of fourteen, twelve of whom are men.

Mission

Guided by the teachings of St. John Bosco and of the Catholic Church, Pacific Technical Centre offers young men of all faiths who have not succeeded in regular secondary school to become capable citizens equipped with technical skills, personal skills, and attitudes fit to meet the challenges of everyday life in a developing economy.

Curriculum

The Centre provides a four year programme of study in design and technology associated with woodwork, metalwork, plumbing, mechanical engineering and boat building. Each technology provides instruction in both the theory and the practical applications and methods associated with the field as well as the range of career possibilities within it. In addition, students are offered a solid base in mathematics, communication skills, fa'asamoa, or cultural education, basic literacy, and religious education. The Centre seeks to develop in its students the virtues of honesty, integrity, responsibility, trust and loyalty, and strives to foster commitment towards the religious and moral convictions which provide the foundation upon which they will grow, learn, advance and adapt as adults.

Overall, the curriculum is holistic, focusing on skills development for employment, livelihood education, continuing education, cultural continuity and the important attitudes and values for lifelong learning. The curriculum aims at enabling students to be productive citizens through having the knowledge, skills and values for paid employment, through fostering traits, behaviours and processes to create self-employment and income generating activities, or through raising achievement to enable them to continue with further studies at Samoa Polytechnic. This is achieved through a close integration of life skills, skills for work, and functional literacy and numeracy.

Student intake and costs

Students are mainly from the rural villages of the two largest islands, Upolu and Savaii. They are boys who have not succeeded in the secondary school system because the could not cope with the demands of an academic curriculum.

Being a non-government institution, the Centre's operation relies heavily on tuition fees to sustain its operation. Tuition costs 360 tala (about $140.00US) per year. Many students are unable to meet this amount so the school organises fund raising activities to supplement school fees in addition to government and donor assistance. Despite these attempts, around 5 per cent of each year's intake is unable to continue because they cannot pay the fees.

Student outcomes

With its aim of enabling students to find employment, develop skills to generate income, or even to continue with further studies, the Centre operates a flexible arrangement whereby students may exit on finding employment which is usually at the insistence of parents. Students who remain at the Centre for the full four years have a very high rate (90%) of success in terms of finding employment or continuing with further studies.

Achievement in mainstream regular school

Reported achievement in mainstream secondary schools was clustered around six areas. In order of most frequent to least frequent, these were:

- personal skills included self management skills, interpersonal skills, leadership roles and spiritual growth

- sports achievements included knowledge and skills to play rugby, soccer, volleyball, athletics, and participate in competitions

- language and literacy, including English proficiency and basic literacy

- cultural proficiency which included knowledge and skills to perform traditional functions such as acknowledging contributions, speech making, and performing traditional dances

- general subject knowledge and examination oriented achievement such as rank in class, eligibility to sit examinations, and awards such as certificates.

Table 1 opposite shows the frequencies of each of the areas. Given that one of the main reasons the students have ended up at Pacific Technical Centre is their low attainment in academic studies, it is not surprising that the boys' least frequently identified areas of achievement were general subject knowledge and examination-based achievement.

Barriers to achievement in mainstream schools

Eleven groups of factors were identified by the students as barriers to their achievement in mainstream schools. In order of most frequent to least frequent these were:

- teacher factors
- home factors
- own attitudes and behaviours
- girl related factors
- school rules and punishment
- language and literacy
- drugs
- peer pressure
- school management,
- attitudes and behaviour of others
- resources.

Aspects	Frequency				
	Rural Schools	Urban School	Totals	%	% by sub-categories
1. Personal skills				28	
a. self management skills	29	21	50	17	
b. interpersonal skills e.g. communication, fellowship, respect	12	9	21	7	
c. leadership roles	8	-	8	3	
d. spiritual growth	4		4	1	
2. Sports	49	26	75	25	25
3. Language and literacy					20
a. English proficiency	13	24	37	12	
b. Basic literacy in Sam/Eng	16	6	22	7	
4. Cultural proficiency	21	16	37	12	12
5. General subject knowledge	13	8	21	7	7
6. Exam oriented achievement					8
a. Rank in class eg 1st – 3rd	4	6	10	3	
b. Eligibility for national exam	6	3	9	3	
c. Certificate	2	2	4	1	
TOTAL	177	121	298	100	100

Table 1 Reported achievements in mainstream secondary schools

The most frequently identified barriers, totalling 42 per cent, were to do with teachers. They included teachers' attitudes, inadequate pedagogy, and too few members of staff. Teacher attitudes were characterised by a disrespect for the dignity of the students through cruel use of corporal punishment, threatening language, put downs, favouritism and lack of attention to weak students. They reported:

> The abuse of students through words and physical punishment... Words that discourage your spirit, that put you down as a person, words that threaten you ... A disregard for your personal dignity...

Pedagogy was described as narrow, uninspiring, not providing feedback or review, and failing to provide differential learning for varied abilities.

> My mind just goes to sleep just sitting and listening to the teacher. Many times when the teacher goes over a subject (he/she) just goes straight through without going back. Does not take account of weak students ... Looks down on weak students...

The most frequently identified home factor was poverty – cash being poor so unable to pay school fees and meet other school costs.

> It is difficult because the fees are high but my family is economically poor.

Self attitudes and behaviours clustered around mental, social and spiritual well-being. Girl factors included views of girls as distracting from studies, shyness and fear of being ridiculed in front of girls, and a lack of relationship skills.

> The relation to girls caused me to be shy to speak for fear of being ridiculed for my lack of abilities. I feel really low.

Table 2 outlines the detailed breakdown of the factors boys considered to contribute to their underachievement in mainstream schools.

■ Proficiency in English language

The students' vocabulary levels based on their scores on the English vocabulary test are shown in Table 3. The results show that 92 per cent (85 out of 92) of all the students in the sample are working below the first 2000 words of English, which is the target requirement for Year 9, the entry year at secondary schools. What is even more significant is that most of these students had spent three or four years at secondary schools. The results indicate that these students had entered secondary schools with a huge deficit in the English they needed for learning and that in their years at secondary school they had still not made up this deficit by the time they left. The results for the first year students for example, show 53 per cent or 20 students working below the first 400 words of English. When you add this to the number of those operating at Level 3 (less than 750 words), this becomes 79 per cent. In other words, 79 per cent of the sampled first year students at Pacific Technical had left secondary schools knowing less than 750 words of English. This would have severely hampered their ability to participate and learn through English.

The results by the third year suggest that after two years at Pacific Technical, the students' vocabulary increased because more students are at

Table 2: Reported barriers to boys' achievement in mainstream schools

Aspects	Rural Schools	Urban Schools	Totals	%	% Totals by category
1. Teacher factors					**42**
a. cruelty, harsh corporal punishment	28	17	45	13	
b. threatening language	11	4	15	4	
c. put downs	8	2	10	3	
d. disrespectful of personal dignity of students	3	3	6	2	
e. puts fear in students	4	2	6	2	
f. impatience with weak students	1		1	0	
g. inadequate content knowledge	8		8	2	
h. favouritism e.g. bright students	2	1	3	1	
i. no attention to weak students	2		2	1	
j. uncaring	1		1	0	
k. no commitment	6		6	2	
l. not enough teachers	8	5	13	4	
m. limited pedagogy: narrow methods, unclear explanations, no feedback, no freedom of expression	20	5	25	7	

Table 2: Reported barriers to boys' achievement in mainstream schools (continued)

Aspects	Rural Schools	Urban Schools	Totals	%	% Totals by category
2. Home factors					17
a. Poverty – cash poor resulting in no school fees, no transport fare, no exam fees, unable to meet other contributions to school	35	10	45	13	
b. conflict	4	2	6	2	
c. family events	5	1	6	2	
3. Self attitudes and behaviours					13
a. limited mental capacity and knowledge	2	1	3	1	
b. unhappy most of the time	1		1	0	
c. shy to seek help for fear of being ridicule	6	3	9	3	
d. absenteeism	3	2	5	1	
e. confrontational behaviours	4		4	1	
f. lack of application		5	5	1	
g. limited skills for learning including self-management skills	4	1	5	1	
h. poor decision making	3	1	4	1	
i. off task behaviours	1	4	5	1	
j. limited coping skills with life changes like puberty	2		2	1	
k. limited spiritual grounding	1		1	0	

Table 2: Reported barriers to boys' achievement in mainstream schools (continued)

Aspects	Rural Schools	Urban Schools	Totals	%	% Totals by category
l. low self esteem due to limited literacy skills	1		1	0	
m. dislike of teachers	2		2	1	
4. Girl factors					**9**
a. attraction to girls	6	6	12	4	
b. fear of being ridicule	9	4	13	4	
c. lack of relationships skills	3		3	1	
5. School rules and punishment					**6**
a. cruel and unreasonable punishments		8	8	2	
b. hard labour	1	3	4	1	
c. too many rules	3		3	1	
d. staying away when rules are broken	3	5	5	1	
6. Language and literacy factors					**4**
a. inadequate English proficiency	3	3	6	2	
b. inadequate literacy skills	4	4	8	2	
7. Drugs					**3**
a. smoking	2	3	5	1	
b. marijuana	1	1	2	1	
c. alcohol	2	2	4	1	

Table 2: Reported barriers to boys' achievement in mainstream schools (continued)

Aspects	Rural Schools	Urban Schools	Totals	%	% Totals by category
8. Peer pressure	4	4	8	2	2
9. School management					2
a. management styles		3	3	1	
b. school environment		3	3	1	
10. Attitudes and behaviour of others					1
a. bullying	2		2	1	
b. name calling	1		1	0	
c. fighting in school	1		1	0	
11. Resource factors					1
a. inadequate resource facilities	4	1	5	1	
TOTALS	117	84	342	100	100

Table 3: Students' vocabulary levels

Numbers from each year level	Below Level 3 100-200 word levels	Level 3 400-750 word levels	Level 4 751-1100 word levels	Level 5 1100-1500 word levels	Level 6 1501-2000 word levels	Over level 6 Focus on university word list	TOTALS
First year students	20	10	2	1	5		38
Second year students	4	12	5	4	6		31
Third year students			4	6	6	7	23
TOTALS	24	22	11	11	17	7	92
%	26	24	12	12	18	8	

Table 4: Sated objectives for being at Pacific Technical

Goals	Rural	Urban	Total	Percent
To serve the family through having a job to improve quality of life, to be of service to village and church, to improve the quality of life for family.	52	32	84	59
To get a job	15	6	21	15
Develop skills in particular technologies	16	3	19	13
Become a qualified tradesperson	2	8	10	7
Be self sufficient, set up a business	5	3	8	6
Be a role model to others		1	1	1
TOTALS	90	53	143	100

Levels 5 and 6 by their third year. However this would have to be verified against baseline data.

Schooling at Pacific Technical Centre
Goals

Whilst at the Centre, the students' goals were mostly directed at achieving the means for improving family livelihoods. Almost 60 per cent of the students expressed their aims in terms of being able to get a job so they could take care of or be of service to the family, village and church. There is a strong sense of paying back a debt to parents for the care and expenses they had met over the years. In addition, there is a strong sense of service to the village and the church. Table 4 shows the goals as identified by the students.

> To improve my future prospects so that I can take care of my family, village and church.

> To finish schooling successfully so that i can get a job to try and pay back my parents money they used on me.

> I aim to be able to look after big jobs, and to establish my own business.

Achievements

Table 5 shows what students considered they had achieved from attending the Centre. It is evident from the frequency distributions that students considered their experiences at Pacific Technical developed the whole person. While technical knowledge and skills had increased, these were complemented by improvements in attitudes, values and life skills. In addition, there was acknowledgement of achievements in language and literacy, religious knowledge and application, and workplace skills.

> I know how to work with timber, metal, and different parts and kinds of timber. I have understanding of the different technologies and skills in carpentry, welding, engineering and others.

The knowledge and skills in technologies have further contributed to an ability to build and repair as required around the family home.

> There are lots of things I can now do for my family like building a food safe, repairing cars, repairing furniture, repairing leaks.

Table 5: Reported achievements at Pacific Technical Centre

Aspects	Frequency	Subtotals	%
1. Increase in knowledge and skills of various technologies	109	109	**30**
2. Attitudes, Values, Behaviours		93	**26**
a. enjoy going to school, look forward to	11		
b. no absenteeism	2		
c. focused, engaged, improved application, honest efforts	13		
d. a sense of freedom to be self	7		
e. desire or keenness to learn	14		
f. purposefulness – having a sense of purpose, a sense of pride in one's achievement	11		
g. mature attitudes and approach	4		
h. positive changes in behaviours and attitudes including affirmation of their dignity and sense of self	21		
i. disciplined lifestyle	10		
3. Life skills		70	**19**
a. self efficacy	8		
b. self sufficiency in home environment	12		
c. cooperation, team work	3		
d. group fellowship	9		
e. interpersonal skills	15		
f. confidence in group, class, whole school communication	21		
g. work ethics	2		

Table 5: Reported achievements at Pacific Technical Centre (continued)

Aspects	Frequency	Subtotals	%
4. Improved language and literacy skills		24	7
a. English	14		
b. Samoan	8		
c. Both	2		
5. Performing arts skills	16	16	4
6. Sports	14	14	4
7. Religious knowledge and application	8	8	2
8. Cultural knowledge and skills	11	11	3
9. Long-boat knowledge skills values	10	10	3
10. Increase in workplace skills	6	6	2
TOTALS	361	361	100

Attitudes were positive. The students were clearly pleased to be at Pacific Technical. They enjoyed going to school and this improved their application to work and giving it their honest efforts. They described a sense of purposefulness, a keenness to learn and a disciplined lifestyle. Many thought that there were positive changes to their outlook and behaviour which stemmed from an affirmation of their dignity. There was a sense of pride in what they had been able to achieve. Overall, the boys' discourse conveys that an important part of their achievements at the school was a reawakening and fostering of their sense of self, a desire to try harder, to be productive and make a contribution to family and village, and to seek further knowledge and understanding in order to do so.

> I like to come [to school]. It has increased my desire to work, to seek further knowledge, to try harder.

> You wake up in the morning and you are keen to come, you look forward to the day ahead and the programme for the day.

> I am able to be of use to my family through the things I can make with my hands.

> My parents are able to view what I am able to do at school.

Students also cited enhanced life skills as being important achievements. In particular they mentioned communication skills and many speak of their increased confidence to interact in group, class and whole school situations with audiences of different ages.

> I have courage and confidence, no longer fearful of speaking in front of people.

Interpersonal skills were frequently highlighted as important aspects of achievement. They include knowing how to behave in relation to others, cooperation and team work.

> I know how to manage my behaviour in relation to others and working together with other boys and teachers.

Developing self-reliance and independence was a proud achievement noted in relation to being able to design and follow through a project to its completion and working without supervision.

> I can do my own work without the teacher. I am able to design and work through a project from my own mind.

Other achievements they mentioned were in cultural knowledge, performing arts, religious knowledge, as well as the knowledge, skills and values associated with racing the long boats. The long boats or *fautasi* were the traditional means of transport between islands or around the coastal villages of an island. Each boat has around 50 rowers and they are now used primarily in competitions during national celebrations. *Fautasi* are owned and rowed by village men. No other school has rowed a *fautasi* during the national competitions, whereas Pacific Technical has rowed twice in one year. The student rowers were extremely proud to have been selected and highlighted this as being a great achievement. The opportunity to row brought many other benefits in terms of knowledge of the science and cultural principles involved in boat design. These included the art and skills of rowing, the discipline involved in maintaining fitness, the fellowship of working as a team, making the school proud, and making monetary contributions to the school through winning prize money.

Overall one gets a sense that in the time they have been at Pacific Technical these boys have become proud achievers. This has been manifest in growing in maturity, living disciplined lifestyles as 'educated' people, being assured about who they are and affirmed through making a productive contribution to their own growth and the livelihoods of their families.

> I have learnt to live as an 'educated' person; I have increased as a person with a mature mind, spiritually, disciplined and able to think through properly for the future.

Effective approaches

Seven key factors at Pacific Technical were identified by students as instrumental to their achievements:

the school environment
school leadership, attitudes, philosophy
the nature of the curriculum
educating for life
teachers' attitudes and philosophy
teacher's pedagogical knowledge and skills,
teacher-student relationship.

The first four of these areas accounted for 80 per cent of the responses. There was a high degree of consistency in the way the students thought about the contributing factors and what teachers in the sample reported. Table 6 (page 94-95) shows the components of each contributing factor.

The school environment

The students identified the aspects of the school environment that they thought contributed to their achievement. A number of factors stand out. The first is the importance to them of the way in which the school values, affirms and nurtures the individual person's dignity. The school does this in a range of ways, including:

- Allowing students a voice through respectful and meaningful dialogue between teachers and students, Principal and students, students and students.

    Pacific Technical takes a very close look at the development of each student. There is freedom in the interaction of students and teachers. The students are encouraged to have their say and are affirmed in their achievements. (Teacher)

    I am able to express what I think without fear of being ridiculed.

- Providing opportunities for students self expression through independent work from design to implementation, setting indicators and self evaluating.

- Making relationships a focal point in the teachings and practices of the school including the spiritual relationship with God, relationships with each other, with family, with teachers, and among the whole school as a community.

    This school works hard to strengthen the boys' spiritual lives and their dignity as people because we believe if they are rooted in spirituality and self dignity they will be well equipped to cope with any future plans. (Teacher)

- Teaching skills for building self awareness, including skills for self-assessment, identifying personal strengths and weaknesses and setting short and long term goals; skills for building self-image and body image, skills for building identity as males.

Table 6: Effective approaches at Pacific Technical Centre

Approaches	Total	Subtotal	% of Subtotals
1. School environment		85	21
a. the importance of the person, dignity self esteem building	21		
b. the importance of the collective, team spirit, school pride	16		
c. behaviour management that uses humour, non-confrontational, uses reinforcement, praise and affirmation	8		
d. encouraging a sense of belonging	7		
e. setting challenges	7		
f. peaceful happy but disciplined school environment	7		
g. class and school cohesion	7		
h. no corporal punishment	6		
i. focus on and celebrating achievement and meeting set targets eg parents' day	3		
j. rules and consequences are explained and based on reasonable principles, fairness	2		
k. having role models	1		
2. School leadership, attitudes, philosophy		83	21
a. challenges and counsels, motivates whole school	32		
b builds a school spirit based on reasoning, kindness, highlights the importance of personal dignity	19		
c. caring	17		
d. humour, calmness	7		
e. high expectations of individuals	5		
f. encourages achievement in various forms	3		

Table 6: Effective approaches at Pacific Technical Centre (continued)

Approaches	Total	Subtotal	% of Subtotals
3. Nature of the curriculum		77	19
a. theory and practical combination	21		
b. religious dimension	13		
c. scope of technologies offered	10		
d. inclusion of performing arts and culture	10		
e. work experience	8		
f. extra curricula eg long boat racing, public performances	8		
g. sports	4		
h. market opportunities for products	3		
4. Educating for life		74	18
a. life skills, values, self worth, self determination, efficacy	33		
b. focus on maleness	17		
c. disciplined lifestyles, decision making	13		
d. work ethics, being productive	11		
5. Teacher Attitudes and Philosophy		34	8
a. calm, cheerful disposition, humour	8		
b. high expectations	6		
c. counsel	6		
d. motivation	4		
e. caring	3		

The students described three key strategies the school uses for building self awareness and relationships. One is the annual school retreat, in which the entire school goes off island or out of the school campus for a week during the first holidays in May-June. It is a time of reflection, building on self esteem, building inter-personal relations and school spirit. The boys spoke fondly of the retreat as a time when teachers and students build each other up, as well as a time of making decisions through shared involvement. It is also a time of conflict resolution in a non-confrontational way. Last but not least, there is also time to have fun.

The second strategy the boys valued is the regular meetings with the whole school, at which the Principal challenges, motivates and counsels the boys, particularly concerning their goals, planning, and self management skills. An important function of these meetings is to build the boys' self esteem and reinforce an environment of care and concern for their wellbeing.

> At these meetings Father talks to us about thinking ahead and living in peace with each other. We are challenged and advised to live sensibly towards our goals. He encourages us to persevere and to do our best.

The third strategy is students' participation in out of school events where they are amongst the public. Such events include competing in the *fautasi* races during national celebrations, performing traditional dances during the celebrations and having sports teams in the local competitions. Participation in these events stressed the importance of the school as a collective. It developed school coherence and cooperation, with the overall effect of building pride in the school. In turn, this pride achieved with the school imbued pride in themselves as a person, and a sense of belonging.

> I was very happy we were placed in the boat race and felt proud for our school but also for me, I know how to row a *fautasi* and lent a hand to school projects.

Focusing on achievement also does much to build the self esteem and self image of students. On Parents' Day and market days, the products of students' projects are on display as evidence of learning and outcomes that they had achieved.

96

Other contributions to the school's environment that the boys noted as supportive were the ban on corporal punishment, that rules and the consequences of breaking them are explained, and that they have role models in their teachers and school leaders.

School leadership, attitudes and philosophy

Students commented often on the importance of the attitudes and philosophy of the school leadership in making them feel accepted, motivated and challenged. As well as the whole school meetings between the Principal and the boys, the school leadership team builds the school spirit through strengthening individual students' dignity. The students felt cared for because the Principal shows them that he cares and tells them so. He lets them know he has high expectations of them. The students reported that he often uses humour in their interactions and felt that this significantly adds to an environment that makes them relaxed and able to interact comfortably with him. In sum, the students believed the school leadership's attitudes and philosophy about discipline and their valuing and respecting of the individual while creating a cohesive school have helped them to learn and motivated them to do their best.

It's the Principal's talk about our dignity, advice and encouragement – he uses humour but you can sense his expectations for the boys.

The curriculum

Most of the students aim to acquire skills for employment and income generation to assist their families. Given their past underachievement in mainstream schools, Pacific Technical has responded with a curriculum that develops not only employment skills but the whole person. Both students and teachers clearly consider the combination of theory, practical and workplace experience as an effective approach. If that were all, the school would lose what appears to be the edge it has. But in addition, it attends to the spiritual dimension of students' lives, continues Samoan language and culture instruction, provides opportunities for dance and visual arts, sports and extra curricula activities. Integrated in all the provision is character building and education for life.

Pacific Technical takes a very close look at the whole development of each student ... Despite the low achievement of boys we do let them know what *they can become ... We encourage them to perform well and participate in other activities outside of school.* (Teacher)

Educating for life

The teachers in the sample reported that, in addition to the courses in technologies, the school prepares the students for the whole of their lives. It incorporates life skills and values into their lessons as well as covering them in the planned school retreats and meetings, courses in religious education, Samoan language and culture, sports and performing arts. The life skills that were considered most important were included in the programmes. These entailed:

- Interpersonal skills: active listening, assertion and refusal skills, negotiation and conflict management, cooperation and team work, and language and literacy skills

- Skills for building self awareness: self assessment, skills for building self image and body image, skills for building identity as males

- Values clarification: understanding gender related issues, understanding different norms, beliefs, cultures, tolerance, diversity

- Decision making skills: critical, creative thinking and problem solving skills, analytical skills for assessing (personal and other) risks, skills for generating alternatives, information gathering skills

- Coping and stress management skills: self control skills, coping with peer pressure, time management skills, skills for dealing with anxiety, for dealing with difficult situations and for seeking help.

There is a high degree of consistency between the skills listed and what the students reported they had achieved. Often they referred to themselves as '*ua ola a'oa'oina, ola pulea*' – living 'educated' disciplined lives as result of life skills education.

The teachers' attitudes and philosophy

The teachers were caring. The students reported that teachers showed they cared by:

- seeking them out when they are not at school, finding out why and going out of their way to ensure they return to full participation
- listening to what they have to say, allowing them a voice
- believing we can make something of ourselves, expecting it
- allowing them to design and complete their own projects
- supporting them with their personal problems
- seeking opportunities for their involvement in public events
- supporting them in co-curricula activities e.g. camping with students for three weeks in preparation for the long boat race
- following up after a difficult personal time
- organising retreats, trips, fund raising
- visiting during workplace experience to reassure them
- standing up for them in conflict situations e.g. inter-school tensions
- seeking markets for their products
- seeking employment opportunities
- teaching them to read and write
- developing their spiritual lives and making wise decisions

Like the school leaders, the teachers believed in the students and in their abilities to be self sufficient. Enhancing their self esteem and self efficacy was a role teachers saw to be as much a part of their work as teaching the theory and practice of various technologies.

> They desire for us [to do well], to live planned and determined lives, to seek after a quality future. They encourage us to live safe lives making good decisions that enhance our dignity.

The teachers' pedagogical knowledge and skills

What was frequently remarked on was the teachers' attention and empathy towards students with weak basic literacy and numeracy skills. Students also spoke about their appreciation for the opportunity to think on their own through designing and making their own projects. They felt the teachers were able to make their subjects easy to understand, and the use of Samoan language assisted a great deal, helping them to understand the English terminology as well. The teachers made known the targets and the indicators for their achievement at the start and consistently pointed to these when they gave feedback but also when suggesting the way forward.

Teacher-student relationships

The students were grateful for being able to interact with teachers in a relaxed manner. This is a consequence of allowing them to have a voice in the classrooms and in whole school situations. They also felt their teachers worked with them as a team. As students they felt trusted, and they believed the teachers respected them as individuals.

Notions of masculinity

The philosophies held by the students about masculinity and their identity as a male are outlined in Table 7. There is a strong association between masculinity, service and protector-ship. The boys most often see themselves in a role of service and protector of their parents, sisters, extended family, village and church. This service is in the form of providing for their food needs, shelter, meeting family obligations to the church and the village. This means finding paid employment, working the land or fishing. The relationship to sisters is sacred and seen as a 'feagaiga' or covenant, the 'i'oimata' or 'pupil of the brothers' eye'. This means that as males, their duties are to protect their sisters and to be of service through ensuring there is sufficient food supply and that it is cooked for them, and by doing the chores.

> My life as a male, I serve my parents, church as well as the village. I serve through doing anything, I serve as an untitled man (In Samoan custom, men who are not titled as orators or chiefs serve as untitled men first before they can be titled) caring for my parents, I protect my sisters because they are my covenant. I do all the chores for my family.

> I believe the male stands strong in carrying out the family work such as cultivation and fishing. The male also protects his sister.

> Your face 'burns' at the cooking fires, serving your parents and your sisters as well as the matai (titled person), you are the hands and feet of service, a refuge for your parents or sisters in days to come.

> I am the male [so] I do all the work for our family, I don't want my sisters to bend their knee at the fires, I serve also my parents and help others.

Table 7: Notions of masculinity

Male Identity	Frequency	%
1. in relation to parents: obedience, respect, protection, service	50	25
2. in relation to sisters: respect, protection, service, help with chores	41	20
3. doer of all the chores as part of their role – plantation, cooking	22	11
4. in relation to village and church: service, respect	19	9
5. in relation to character: to be respectful and disciplined	18	9
6. in relation to family – notion of *tausi aiga* – i.e. caregiver, provider, protectorship eg through employment both paid and non waged	14	7
7. as future leadership in workplace, leaders in family, village, planner, adviser, the right hand person	20	10
8. genders working in partnership, dialogue	8	4
9. peace maker in family, in village and church,	4	2
10. go to church	3	1
11. cultural continuity	2	1
12. appointed to national decision making	1	0
TOTALS	**202**	**100**

> I believe the male must get a job to take care of the family – he serves, his face 'burns' at the cooking fires. Although girls seem to have out-perform boys at school, it is the boys' heritage to serve without relying on anyone else.

We can contrast this with the way that Jamaican boys have lost out by doing little housework. The boys do have a desire to serve but see no male models undertaking such tasks. To be fair to Jamaican men, it is often the males in the countryside that come close to adopting a Samoan-like culture. They will cook the jerk-pork, know how to crotchet and yet be skilful with a cutlass.

Masculinity is also associated with leadership, for which service is a pre-requisite. Through service, males can learn to be leaders, be responsible for safeguarding family assets, distributing family resources, and representing the family at village and church forums. There is a strong belief in these masculine identities as being their heritage.

> The male serves parents and sisters; he is the head of the family, the strength of the family, and the pillar of the family in the village and church, he is the decision maker whom everyone listens to.

> The inherited role of the male is to serve the family because one day he will be the leader of the family, village or church. He must be obedient to his parents and be faithful in work and contributions to the village and church because the way to authority is through service.

> Males are appointed as leaders of families and church because males are appointed to make decisions for the country.

> The inheritance of the male is to serve parents and family and he will also be the leader in the future.

It must be stressed that the majority of the boys are from the rural villages in Samoa, where tradition is strong. The school seems to reinforce these notions through 'making the boys aware of their role in families and society: to become good fathers, *matai* and providers of the family' (teacher). Notions of masculinity are grounded in cultural beliefs and practices that are very much part of life today in the villages.

THE IMPLICATIONS FOR SAMOA AND ITS MEN

The Pacific Technical Centre provides a second chance in education to boys who were failed by mainstream education. The barriers to their achievements highlighted teacher factors, home factors and self related factors as the three most frequently kinds of barriers identified. On the other hand, the students in the sample said that they achieved in many different ways to do with knowledge and skills of various technologies, attitudes, values and behaviours, life skills, language and literacy, spirituality, and workplace skills. Underlying their achievements is a strong sense of dignity and self worth that the school environment has fostered.

The students in the sample endorsed the role of the caring school environment, school leadership attitudes and philosophy, the nature of the curriculum, education for life, teacher attitudes and philosophy, teacher pedagogy and good teacher-student relationships as providing inspiration for their achievements.

5

Change from within: JAMAICA

I f cultural legacy is acknowledged as the root of genius, schools can be powerful engines for transforming the lives of boys who are disadvantaged. However, schools have been resistant to change, especially when the agents for transformation come from outside the institution. An alternative is for the key stakeholders and leaders of schools to work together in the transformation of their schools.

This case study presents the findings of a unique experiment in the Caribbean: Change from Within. Certain primary and secondary school Principals formed a collaborative group to improve their school environments. They faced common problems which were underpinned by the failure of Jamaican boys to succeed in the country's education system. This case study focuses on the following questions:

- ■ What approaches, local and international, have been taken to tackle the issue of male underachievement?

- ■ What has been the impact specifically on Jamaican boys to date?

- ■ What were the origins of the Change from Within project?

- ■ Why was it successful?

- ■ How have schools applied the Change from Within process in their schools?

- ■ What should schools be doing to make education more engaging for Jamaican boys?

Change from Within used qualitative methods and multiple techniques of data gathering: that is, semi-structured interviews with key informants, analysis of diaries and school records.

The context of male underachievement: poverty and emotional intelligence

Jamaica has one of the highest homicides rates in the world and most of the killings are committed by young men. To deal with the problem of youth violence, education systems in Jamaica and the region have to redefine their role in moulding what should be socially and emotionally well-adjusted young people who are equipped with a well-defined set of personal attributes and a predetermined range of aptitude and skills.

The impact of poverty on many boys' school performance and behaviour should not be minimised, and neither should the lack of aspiration and material resources of parents and the impact of living in communities that are divided. These factors are reinforced by the 'spoiling' of young boys already discussed.

In general, the Jamaican education system has been excessively concerned with academic performance and insufficiently concerned with meeting students' emotional needs. While it is true that parents have a responsibility to nurture children, the reality was that, as a result of their own inadequate socialisation, many parents lacked the skills to perform this critical role. It was often the parents themselves who caused the greatest emotional damage to their youngsters. In this context, the education system has a crucial role to play in fostering emotionally healthy children so the focus can no longer be solely on academic concerns.

Jamaican educators have realised the need to adopt more holistic approaches. Offering opportunities for dance, sport and extra-curricula activity has been the hallmark of its best schools. But with a comprehensive education system that caters for all, schools needed to be aware of the modern global pressures that affect young men. The issue of 'barrel children' exemplified the problem of how many young men not only lacked a father figure but whose mothers were working abroad and had left them in the care of a relative. Young males were arriving at school feeling bitter and frustrated because there was no emotional support at home. They were literally left to fend for themselves. Many did not know how to cope and so withdrew or resorted to violence.

Some schools just reflected the wider society rather than presenting an alternative to it. As a result boys learnt antisocial attitudes at school. The socialisation of males began in the home but it continued in a society that held strong stereotypes about what should constitute male behaviour. Consequently, many teachers might expect the girls to continue their domestic role at school while the boys play.

Young people need praise, validation and demonstrations of love. Being subjected instead to systematic invalidation and other put-downs both at home and at school would severely damage their psyches. Unresolved negative feelings resulting from experiences of early emotional hurt easily lead to antisocial behaviour and even violence.

The origins of Change from Within

Change from Within is a programme of human resource development designed to promote cooperative interaction within schools and involving partnership between schools, communities, organisations and the larger society. Its participatory methodology involved listening to the children and drawing on the resources of self, school and community in the process of development and change. Some of the significant activities undertaken in the schools, and some of the issues and challenges raised as various schools attempted to stimulate and encourage change from within are relevant to this case study.

The programme initially focused on four inner-city schools in Jamaica. It sought to show how Change from Within can become a powerful liberating force, building on self esteem, pride in our ancestry, and in the remarkable record of African-Jamaican historic achievements. Under the inspirational leadership of Sir Phillip Sherlock, the attempt was made to elaborate the Change from Within process and to extend it to schools throughout Jamaica. Over one year, Change from Within, under the management of Pauletta Chevannes, undertook a process of applying the Change from Within process in six schools.

How it was applied in schools

The methodology of the Change from Within programme operated at several levels. First, at a participatory action research level, which involved the engagement in and ownership of the programme by all the constituents: the community, the students, the teachers, the administration, and the parents. This entailed observation, documentation, discussion and analysis. At this level, the methodology allowed for the adjustment of strategies according to how different schools identified their problems. This could mean making changes to procedures in response to the circumstances. There was consequently a certain degree of openness in the procedures so as to allow feedback relating to their particular position. Also at this level, participants were empowered to take the initiative and conceptualise, plan, and implement strategies using a large knowledge base generated by research findings as well as the rich experiences shared during meetings.

At another level, the methodology involved a number of strategies for promoting change and building cooperation, such as:

- creating a general awareness of the process
- building social skills
- establishing positive interdependence
- encouraging supportiveness and building a good interpersonal environment. This required the promotion of positive interactions to create a climate that built morale and self esteem and encouraged respect, trust, and conflict reduction.

At a third level, the methodology included the process of institution building. This involved the 'servicing of the infrastructure' to encourage self help. Workshops, training sessions and meetings served not only to provide guidance and assistance but also to encourage the participants to identify and own the problems and challenges in their schools, to generate workable solutions, map plans for action and implement strategies.

Friendship Group

The friendship group was one of the significant features of the programme: its 'engine'. This group comprised all the Principals, a few teachers selected by their Principals as support persons, and the researchers involved in the project.

The participants held monthly meetings where they updated one another on the progress of activities at their respective schools, sought and exchanged ideas, planned different initiatives and devised strategies for intervention. The group evolved into a committed and dedicated team and exchanged regular observations and suggestions about what was happening at the schools.

They also provided emotional and psychological support and assisted each other in building their self awareness and development – itself a critical aspect of the change process. They helped one another to discover that for the process to work and ultimately to ensure the success of the project, Change from Within must begin with the leader.

Programme development

The significant approaches decided upon had to be identified and articulated in each of the schools, relating, as they did, to the specific challenges that highlighted by the respective schools. The group identified the following objectives:

- parental support and involvement in school activities
- engagement of the communities
- use of self expression and the arts as a means for self improvement, communication and motivation
- guidance and counselling programmes as a means for identifying and solving personal problems
- bad behaviour being seen as a cry for help
- a curriculum rooted in the cultural identity needs of Jamaicans
- sensitivity to the particular needs of male students
- highly trained teaching staff who are committed to the change process
- efficient and effective management techniques and practices/, and ownership by the key stakeholders as a result of consultation and analysis of needs
- a leadership prepared to take risks
- recognising the need to develop children's emotional intelligence.

The challenges

Change from Within recognised the challenge concerning self esteem. Due to their cultural and material environment, many children are made to feel virtually worthless. So for effective and positive change to take place it was necessary to develop the students' self esteem. This would mean overcoming a number of challenges.

The first was a cultural one. Students were no longer influenced by traditional Caribbean lifestyles. Rather, there were new issues to contend with, such as globalisation, information technology and materialism, all of which contributed to a change in values.

The second challenge was the problem of growing violence and indiscipline in schools and communities. This was highlighted by recent severe acts of violence in at least three secondary schools.

The third challenge concerned gender performance, meaning the way in which masculine identities were working themselves through in the current environment, often moving boys away from academic performance and towards other compensatory but negative types of behaviour.

The fourth arose from the current socio-economic environment and the consequent reduction of opportunities for jobs after students graduate. This made alternative lifestyles appear to be more attractive.

One internal challenge was to recognise the wide diversity of approaches to promoting Change from Within. Some of these ways might be informal and go unrecognised or be unfairly stigmatised. The important lesson was that there was no one method for promoting Change from Within and that it was an evolving process that operated at different levels. Different schools responded to local peculiarities in different ways and promoted Change from Within by pursuing their objectives and working with different visions. The process involved a matrix of change working on four levels:

- individual
- parents and home
- the wider community
- the school

These four broad categories resulted in a matrix for change that schools and policy makers could use as a school improvement tool to raise the achievement of boys.

Change from Within: Change the environment and change the boys

The project has responded effectively to the evidence across the region of boys doing badly in school. Although developed in Jamaica, it could be as easily and usefully implemented by schools elsewhere. School-based action research projects showed the two factors that contributed most to the alienation of boys. First was the nature of the early socialisation of boys by parents, their community and school. Second was the 'drill to kill' teaching and learning that has increasingly marginalised boys and many girls in the schooling process. Good practice methods of change have revealed that active learning and radical ways of engaging parents in the education of their children are producing positive outcomes.

The most pressing problems faced by most schools in Jamaica today centre around the male students: violence and other antisocial behaviour, poor attendance, and poor academic performance. The CFW methodology focused on changing the cultural, physical and spiritual environment of the school and making it an enabling one. The guiding philosophy was that positive change would be irreversible if its origin is from *within*. Boys would then want to excel, and would eschew violence and unleash their energy in creative ways if motivated to do so. And the best way of motivating them was by providing them with appropriate inspiration.

The success of CFW can be measured by the extent to which violence in or outside the schools by students, particularly boys, was reduced if not eliminated, and the extent to which boys had been able to hold their own academically.

At the start of the change process, hardly a day passed that the staff of the schools did not have to dress wounds inflicted by children on their peers. But as the change process deepened and the self esteem of the children rose, so the incidence of conflict and violence began to diminish. The successes the change generated gave the school the moral confidence and competence to begin addressing the problem at the root – which, on critical examination, turned out to be the home.

Armed with this knowledge, and forging links with the wider community, in this case the community police and the Courts, the leadership set about a programme of educating parents. The children too, became trainers of their own parents. So successful have these efforts been that the violence has been eliminated from the case study school altogether. It is now alien to the culture of the school. And the leadership has oriented the staff and its external support to become the providers of services to parents in need.

Group meetings

The group of Principals, a few support staff and the research team met once a month to share experiences and ideas, plan strategies for action, and learn how to improve skills of leadership. A total of eight meetings were held. These were central to the participatory methodology and facilitated effective feedback and communicative planning. They allowed for strategies to be adjusted in light of how different schools identified their problems so that changes could be made to procedures in response to the immediate circumstances. The meetings were characterised by openness and willingness to respond to feedback and the experiences of others. The effectiveness of Change from Within is illustrated with the example of a primary school.

St John's Primary school
Initial problems and challenges

Located in one of the most violent and poverty stricken areas in Jamaica, the school was characterised by:

- the low self esteem of the students and community
- the impact on students of community violence
- the teachers' low morale and lack of motivation

Mrs Bolt assumed leadership of St Johns Primary school in1988. She described the situation as reflecting what was happening in the area around the school. Specifically, the students displayed violent behaviour, indiscipline, low morale, a lack of social grace and a negative attitude to work. Attendance was very poor. In fact, only half the 300 students on roll attended school regularly. The children who did attend were seen as 'rejects' whose parents thought 'would not come to anything'. They came mainly from depressed communities such as Bennett Land, Sea View Gardens and Water House.

Mrs Bolt said it was common for students to 'stab each other, mostly with pencils'. Funds and time were expended on first aid supplies and dressing wounds. The students' behaviour was appalling, for example students would defecate on the floors or in the bathroom instead of in the toilets. She later learned that such behaviour sprang from the students' home situations – many homes had no toilet.

Making a start

Mrs Bolt took on the challenge to transform St Johns. Her motivation was partly derived from the fact that she saw the students as 'beautiful clean children, who just needed help'. The first years of the transformation process were spent trying to change the behaviour of the students and their negative attitude to work and school.

She soon realised that for any change to succeed it was necessary to share her vision of change with everyone involved. So she sought the input of the teachers, parents and the community as a whole. 'Reaching the teachers' was especially important, as she realised from a conversation she had with grade six students. She cited a touching comment from one of the girls as greatly motivating her to initiate change in the school.

In the conversation she asked a group of boys: 'Why is it that you are always getting into trouble, fighting with each other, being rude to teachers and performing so poorly?' At first, no one responded, and then a little girl spoke up, 'Miss, they won't tell you but I will. Every day you mother say to you that you naw come to nuttin, and you come to school and teacher say the same thing, so why should we try to do better miss?'

Mrs Bolt realised then that to achieve any serious change in the behaviour or performance of the children she would have to deal with the teachers first. She emphasised the difficulty of this task and described the process of communicating with them as like 'communicating with a wall'. The cultural barriers which manifested themselves in low

111

morale and motivation were difficult to penetrate and Mrs Bolt had to try various methods in her quest to cultivate a shift in ways of thinking and generate acceptance, motivation and enthusiasm about change. Some teachers thought she 'was crazy', some resigned, but those who replaced the ones who left 'came with new ideas and were willing to move with me'.

Community involvement was an important part of the process. Mrs Bolt and her team of teachers visited the surrounding communities with the aim of selling their ideas and vision, becoming acquainted with the social and physical condition of the communities. Mrs Bolt told me, 'It was an eye opener to discover many homes had dirt on the floors and that large numbers of persons used one bathroom'. What the teachers learnt helped them to understand some of the problems that the students were faced with on a daily basis. These insights evoked empathy and they were now armed with facts that would enable them to help the pupils more effectively.

Introducing Change from Within

Mrs Bolt welcomed the Change from Within programme into the school in 1990 – an opportune time, as it supported and added value to the work she was undertaking. This new initiative was a joint project between the University of the West Indies and the St Johns School, headed by the late Sir Phillip Sherlock. The aim was to reduce violence among students and to enhance identity and self esteem.

The guiding philosophy was that in order to change behaviour, the environment in which students operated must also be changed. This meant not only the physical surroundings or particular location but also the social and psychological variables which engendered or shaped values and attitudes and were institutionalised as part of the culture. 'Environment' also referred to the personal attributes and attitudes individuals develop out of interaction with their socio-cultural circumstances.

The Change From Within concept added value and a firm thrust to Mrs Bolt's own efforts. The University was instrumental in providing workshops and seminars for the teachers, geared towards staff development and motivation.

Building the team

The initial change process produced both positive and negative effects. It de-motivated some of the teachers, causing a number to resign – in one instance, five teachers resigned at once. Mrs Bolt took the opportunity however, to pursue a special recruitment drive where she sought 'new blood that was talented and shared the new vision for the school', and thus create a team of highly motivated, trained teachers, who were willing to 'go the extra mile' for students.

Initiating behavioural changes: the hug technique

As simple as it may appear, Mrs Bolt found that one of the most effective tools for initiating behavioural changes in the students was a simple hug or a touch. She still sees a hug as 'an energy pill' and she found it quite natural to interact with students in this way. She had acquired the habit of hugging students while teaching at the Norman Manley Comprehensive High School and it had, she declared, proven quite effective in 'reaching students', and that they normally responded by 'performing well to get a hug'. She implied that she had found a correlation between hugs and students' performance.

The Principal extended the 'hug concept' to the teachers and parents too. At the Parent Teachers Association (PTA) meetings, parents were encouraged and taught how to hug their children. As she said, 'By touching, the students became more humane and appreciative of each other. And now ... everybody hugs'. Mrs Bolt believes that hugging and touching were important in changing behavioural tendencies among the students. The students learned to appreciate each other and this undermined the existing culture of violence.

Music

Mrs Bolt believed it was important to use the limited resources they had – of the school, the teachers and the students themselves – as a means of inculcating positive attitudes towards learning. Music was used to spark the interest of students who were listless and showed little interest in learning. Her impression was that 'many of them were illiterate, but they knew the popular songs and they had good memories'. Students would sing songs of artists such as Bob Marley, Jimmy Cliff and Tony Rebel, and then teachers would guide discussions about the lyrics. Students were enthusiastic about this method of learning, and teachers took the opportunity to teach poetry reading, drama and art through the medium of music. The St Johns Ensemble was created out of this musical experiment.

Today, the choir is vibrant and active, and gives performances locally and internationally. Mrs Bolt sought to use opportunities provided by the recognition of events in the calendar such as Black History Month, Heritage Week and Easter to highlight positive themes and instil positive values in the students. For example, during Black History Month, she emphasised the theme: 'Looking into self' as a means of fostering positive self awareness. National symbols and figures were also used to good effect.

Case material: Percival

Mrs Bolt cited the case of Percival, an aggressive and mischievous 10-year-old boy with a poor attendance record. Traditional punishments were first employed in the attempt to change Percival's attitude, such as being sent out of class, being sent to the Principal's office and having to participate in community service, but they seemed to have little effect. To get the him to explain the reasons for his behaviour, Mrs Bolt embarked on a one-to-one conversation with young Percival. She sought to link his name with that of the Prime Minister so he saw it as a mark of importance or status, and told him that the Prime Minister was once a 'little boy' who grew up to occupy his present position.

Prior to this conversation, young Percival was totally unaware that he shared his first name with the Prime Minister. He was clearly elated, appearing to find it interesting and stimulating that his name was so respectable and distinguished.

Mrs Bolt reported that this seemed to have sparked a sense of responsibility and self esteem in Percival, as there were noticeable changes in his behaviour and attitude to school. His attendance improved, and in cases where he expected to be absent, he called to let her know that he would not be attending classes. With a better attendance record, his reading ability improved significantly and Percival will be promoted from the 'Special Class' to the regular grade six group in the next school year.

At present, the school is supporting Percival's change by means of assistance through the school feeding programme and personalised monitoring of his progress by his teachers and the Principal.

Mentoring

Mentoring has been useful in fostering proper guidance for students. When an 'unruly' student was asked who he saw as a role model or most admired, he identified another student whom Mrs Bolt considered to be a bright and disciplined boy. So she called the 'role model' and instructed him to take the 'unruly' student under his care and supervision, whereupon complaints about his bad behaviour diminished significantly. So did his visits to her office for punishment. Instead he now visits her frequently to offer his assistance for anything she might need. Note that the role models here are not strangers but peers. Role modelling always works best with someone the child knows.

Exposure

Mrs Bolt related that she occasionally assigned tasks to different groups of students that involved conducting some form of research which was usually unrelated to the curriculum. She once told a group of grade six students to visit a financial institution and select one of the processes done on a daily basis – such as opening an account – learn about it and report the findings to their classmates. Another time, she assigned a group of grade four students to find out about the history of the school. She said that this broadened their scope of knowledge and that it also provided much needed 'exposure' to make them better individuals. She said that the students have expressed their liking and appreciation of these activities.

Analysing social problems

An interactive approach to analysing social problems affecting students meant that teachers found themselves having unplanned discussions with students about matters that affected them on a daily basis. For example, from time to time teachers engaged the students in discussions about current affairs such as crime and violence in Jamaican society today – which affected many of the students' communities.

Mrs Bolt mentioned a case which drew the attention of most of the students: a body was found in a garbage disposal area in the community. She used the opportunity to brief them about critical issues relating to violence. One grade two teacher said she sometimes used the approach of asking the students about the news in order to engage them in discussions on critical social issues. She added, 'It is rather amazing how much they know; they are very aware and knowledgeable about a lot of issues'.

Clubs and the sustaining of change

Presently, the clubs at the school serve as the conduit through which change is facilitated and engendered. The names, role and functions of these clubs are as follows:

- *Awareness* – increased the awareness of self and the environment by inculcating and promoting positive self image and personal awareness
- *Brownie Pack* – helped the students to develop leadership skills and a culture of offering voluntary service
- *Environment* – served to instil the value and appreciation of a healthy community conducive to enhanced living
- *Club Scout Pack* – instilled discipline and sense of responsibility
- *The Ensemble* – unearthed, developed, trained and exposed the talent of students, so building self esteem and discipline and providing avenues to channel students' energies and positive development in all areas of their lives
- *Builders* – developed leadership potential, to foster the development of strong moral character, encourage loyalty to school, community and nation; and provide opportunities for working together in service to school and community
- *Optimist* – helped students to develop leadership skills. It helped create an orientation for giving service and fostering and encouraging good interpersonal relationships.

Each student was expected to join at least one club. Mrs Bolt said that generally the students were 'hand picked' and placed in specific clubs based on the need of the child, as it related to their behavioural tendencies, performance and social conduct. The students who were placed in the Ensemble for example, were those who generally displayed disruptive and aggressive behaviour. She explained that the choir was formed in order to use music as an avenue for converting the negative energies of these students into positive ones and redirecting talents which were being channelled in destructive rather than constructive ways.

Case study material – Cavel

Cavel's display of unruly behaviour illustrated how students might unintentionally exhibit negative attributes when their talents were not properly channelled. His constant mimicking, mocking and jeering at his teachers and peers caused distraction and annoyance in class. There were frequent complaints from his teachers about his intolerable behaviour. They tried all the usual forms of punishment: asking him to stand at the back of the class, asking him to leave the class temporarily, sending him to the Principal's office where she would ensure that he did community service. As a last resort, Cavel was placed in the choir.

His music teacher reported that Cavel began by being extremely vocal in his usual provocative manner. In an effort to discipline him through embarrassing him, she ordered him to take her place and conduct the class. To her surprise, he seized the opportunity to put on a show, proving his ability not only to mimic but also to articulate effectively. This made the teacher recognise his natural talent in speech and drama and she sought to encourage his development by enabling him to perform.

Cavel entered the Kiwanis Club Public Speaking Competition in 2002, where he won first place in the divisional oratorical contest. He was selected to enter the international competition, where he was placed second. He was also asked to speak at the Kiwanis International Conference in the USA in June 2002. Since his recent achievements, his teachers reported that there had been a dramatic turn-around in Cavel's behaviour. The mimicking and jeering has ceased and he has developed more confidence and self esteem. Mrs Bolt concluded that the *Change from Within* came out of Cavel's needing more attention and wanting to display his natural talents and have them harnessed.

The Ensemble has served its intended purpose of positively influencing the lives of the children who display antisocial behaviour. According to Mrs Bolt and the teachers in charge, there have been noticeable behavioural changes in several students.

In discussions with the group, students said:

> The Ensemble has developed my talents and showed me things that I never believed I could do. It has helped me to go places and meet important people; also it has taught me how to behave in public.

> The Ensemble helps me physically and mentally. I am not afraid to speak with people or to perform in public. I look forward to it. My performance in my school work has improved and I am more willing to participate in class.

In a conversation with the advisor, the Principal – justifiably – boasts:

> The Ensemble is an exceptional group of extremely talented and well exposed students. The group has done a tremendous job in raising the standard of the school, with its limited resources, and has become a trailblazer in the community. It has given some of our needy and less fortunate students hope through the performing arts and has widened the scope of many to excel.

The Ensemble has had a powerful impact on not only the school and the community but also on the country. Every year for the past four years, they have been invited to perform in Canada, where they offer a lively concert of dance, song and drums. A newspaper editorial (*The Gleaner*, March 26, 2002), applauded the students as they 'set out to do Jamaica proud in Ontario'. The writer commended the youngsters and encouraged them to 'keep up the good work.'

Since 1997, the group's achievements have earned them fifteen gold medals, two silver and one bronze in national music festivals, one gold and two silvers in speech competitions and three national trophies. Some clubs have instituted programmes that include and encourage the participation of the entire student body and the teachers. The Builders Club, for example, has introduced the concept of the 'terrific kid', encouraging competition at class level on a combination of factors pertaining to the student's performance, conduct, deportment, attire, relationship with peers and teachers and attitude to the environment. Students who are exemplary in all these areas are nominated by their peers and teachers, and they receive awards from the Kiwanis Club, presented at the General Assembly where they are publicly congratulated by their peers and teachers.

Mrs Bolt said that the 'terrific kid' concept has 'truly served to encourage high performance and exemplary behaviour'. Students are assessed, selected and awarded on a monthly basis. She says that 'everyone wants to become a 'terrific kid', so generally they try to meet the standards required'. Two members of the Builders' club told me how being a member of the club has affected lives.

> The Builders Club teaches me to help others, to share with others who are less fortunate and enables me to cooperate with others. It also teaches me to lead with authority and follow humbly. I am more confident to stand and represent myself and my club and I get a chance to meet people.

> The Builders' Club teaches me how to be a good leader and to face my difficulties with confidence. It also teaches me to be committed to my duties and to represent the club with pride and always look at the bright side of life and improve myself every day.

The Brownie Pack and Cub Scout Pack are single-sex clubs for girls and boys respectively. Both are instrumental in developing leadership skills and discipline in their members. Mrs Bolt said that though students may join voluntarily, some are specifically directed to join, in an effort to curb poor behaviour. She calls some of these students 'ringleaders of trouble'. They display strong leadership qualities that they used to solicit followers whom they led into acts that defied rules and caused trouble. The case of Javon typifies the scenario Mrs Bolt described.

Case material: Javon

The 12 year old grade 6 boy lived with both his parents in the environs of a very violent area in the capital, Kingston. After a few months his parents migrated, reportedly fleeing reprisal from gunmen who accused his father of having murdered a member of the adjoining neighbourhood. Javon was left with his grandmother. This experience caused him obvious social discomfort, emotional stress and a bitterness that manifested itself in antisocial behavioural tendencies.

Javon displayed aggression and violence towards his peers. He was able to manipulate and intimidate other students into behaving in ways that suited him but were contrary to the rules of the school. So he was regularly at the centre of incidents of bad behaviour as the ringleader. Traditional means of punishment were applied but failed to produce any noticeably positive results.

Although it was manifest negatively, Javon's ability to influence others was apparent to Mrs Bolt. She interpreted it as an indication of his desire for attention and a need to redirect his inherent leadership qualities. Her first step towards change was to assign to him leadership responsibilities in the Cub Scouts Pack and other class activities.

This immediately evoked in Javon a more meaningful sense of responsibility and purpose. She emphasised the fact that he attended to his new responsibilities with great seriousness, and performed well in executing the duties assigned to him. She was quick to highlight an incident where the faculty advisor for the Scouts Group turned up late for a meeting, only to learn that because of his lateness (of which Javon seemed to disapprove), Javon had already cancelled the meeting and sent the boys home.

Another notable example arose when group work was assigned in a grade six maths class that required students to solve maths problems as a group, and report the answers to the rest of the class. Whilst the other groups tried to work out or calculate and report the answers all together, Javon assigned different sections of the task to different group members, and designated one individual to report the answer, again demonstrating his leadership and organisational skills.

The teaching staff

The Principal attributed the changes in her students to her team of highly trained, committed and dedicated staff. Over the years, she has managed to facilitate a significant change in attitude and behaviour and has improved morale through staff development workshops and retreats. She boasts that her staff members now take a proactive approach in the process as they seek to foster change within themselves and in the students. In support of her claim, she relates how the members of staff also tend to hold regular workshops on varying topics and issues among themselves, without any instructions from her. These workshops are developed, planned and conducted by the staff themselves and she is usually invited – as a participant or observer.

Mrs Bolt reported that the tutors are also generally willing to attend to individuals' problems and to assume responsibilities and duties which require them to act or serve beyond their regular duties. They tend to volunteer as well as take on new challenges. Recently, she requested a staff team to conduct a workshop for Pembroke Hall High School as a Change from Within initiative. They agreed enthusiastically because they saw it as an opportunity to develop their own competence and confidence. The reviews and evaluations from the teacher at Pembroke Hall who attended the workshop indicated their success in this venture.

The teachers at St Johns appear to be content and motivated. Over the past ten years, staff turnover had been fairly low, except at the end of the August 2001, when five teachers migrated to take up teaching jobs in England and the United States, following a massive recruitment drive in Jamaica for teachers. In discussions with five different teachers, however, the general feelings expressed were that as long as they decided to continue in the profession of teaching, they had no desire to leave St Johns. Mrs Bolt spoke of a teacher who recently resigned because he had to move to another parish. She said he had called her since to discuss the possibility of being re-hired, as he 'missed his school dearly'.

The community

The number of vagrants around the school has declined significantly and Mrs Bolt attributes this to the impact the school has had on the community. The school frequently invited parents and community members to workshops and had over a few years facilitated training programmes as well. Parents and community members were also able to attend these in order to develop marketable skills that would help them to find or create jobs.

To deal with the issue of the vendors, the Principal invited them to sell in a confined area on the school compound. She involves them in the activities of the school by giving them the opportunity to take lead prayers during assembly on some occasions. She noted that a few children still 'hang out' on the streets, but recognised none of them as students of St Johns, past or present.

Conclusion

There is strong evidence to suggest that the best route out of poverty is through education. Parents with higher incomes are in a better position to give their children the social capital they need to succeed. This can range from knowing how to access the best schools to using weekends and summer holidays as times to push their children ahead. Children from less privileged backgrounds lack this advantage.

Child poverty is related to underachievement; there is universal evidence that in competitive situations those who have better diets, healthcare, housing, and access to educational toys, books and private coaching are likely to outperform those who do not. Exceptional people may avoid this trend, but these remain in the minority. Poverty is not an excuse for underachievement but it is a contributory factor towards it. All this was clearly understood by Mrs Bolt.

The real issues for boys were solved at the environmental level at St Johns. Inner-city children were in many ways given access to what their middle class peers regularly receive. The exam results in this school are just as good as any uptown school because of all the out of school activities. The Principal re-modelled her school by providing for the needs of the local community, and giving her children from poor backgrounds the additional education hours to keep them on task. The boys did well in this environment, clearly benefiting from the range of creative activity that the school offers in its extension programme.

Pacific Technical and St Johns primary school illustrate the Generating Genius principles. They exemplified how ritual, love and schooling gave the boys the resilience to learn and to contribute to their school and society. The boys at Pacific Technical were boat makers; like Odysseus they were craftsmen able to turn their hands at most technical challenges. They became problem solvers who worked in a context where their skills were valued.

6

The making of Genius

The human being is the most helpless thing produced by the earth....For as long as the gods give him courage and plant vigour in his limbs, he thinks that he will never come to any harm in the future; when the blessed gods do indeed bring grief upon him, he has to bear it, reluctantly, but with endurance. (*Homer's Odyssey*)

A man should go through tribulation in order to know himself. *Dennis Brown*

No one who can rise before dawn three hundred sixty days a year fails to make his family rich. *Chinese proverb*

Hard fi dead. *Jamaican proverb*

Generating Genius started from a premise that black boys, despite difficult social and family circumstances, were capable of a great deal. This was abundantly clear in the case studies described in the previous two chapters, and thrillingly evident in the outcomes of the Generating Genius Project. This chapter describes the project, beginning with the educational context and debates. It looks at the main principles and describes the methodology they underpinned. Boys on the project give accounts of their experiences in the host universities in England to which the project transported them, and there are comments by boys and parents about the impact of the project.

The project, led by the author and the Pro Vice Chancellor for Graduate studies at the Mona campus of the University of the West Indies (UWI), followed a pilot summer school in Jamaica in 2005. The following year, 25 black boys selected from inner city schools at the age of 12 faced an intellectually challenging three weeks at London University's prestigious Imperial College, exposed to their acclaimed Science, Engineering and Medical departments and tackling work befitting 18-year-olds.

Constructing the project

The programme targeted boys who are just entering the first form or year 7. The Jamaican pilot selected boys from all socio-economic backgrounds who had achieved 90 per cent or over in GSAT Science. The age of 12 was significant, as statistics show that although 60 per cent achieve highly in science related subjects at that age but that this drops to around 20 per cent by the time they reach GCSE/CXC level. So we wanted to tackle this problem and re-establish the boys' earlier passion for science.

Advertisements were placed in the press and in high schools across the island for 20 boys to work at UWI in the summer with 10 boys from the UK. Applicants were asked to write an essay of 250 words on '*Why I want to be a research scientist or a doctor*'. The short-listed applicants were interviewed to assess their suitability for the programme.

Predictably the project drew criticism as well as acclaim. 'Why only boys'? asked the critics. 'And why science?' The account of the project which follows, plus the comments of the students, should go some way to answering these questions.

Why boys?

Much of the book has already answered this question. It is boys who are being failed; it is boys who need help to find the female within; it is boys who most threaten to disrupt society.

In Jamaica the largest University is the Mona campus of the University of the West Indies. In 2007 85 per cent of the new students entering the campus were female. A possible way to explain this is to go back to the different child rearing practices applied to boys and girls. Jamaican researchers Janet Brown and Gayle McGarrity (1997) asked a group of six year olds to list the household chores that they had to perform at home (see opposite).

In reflecting on the differential academic achievement of boys and girls, UWI economist Mark Figueroa (1996) suggests that it is the very pat-

SIX YEAR OLD GIRLS	SIX YEAR OLD BOYS
Clean house	Eat grapes, mangoes, apples
Wipe out house	Stone mangoes
Read books	Feed the puppy scraps
Sweep and mop	
Wash school bag	
Wash plate	
Wash panties (from age 4/5, they said)	
Wash socks	
Wash school uniform	
Clean the toilet	
Cook – fry egg, dumplings, cook rice	
Clean up pig mess	
Comb hair (my own, my mom's)	
Water goat	
Water plants	

terns of early socialisation which produce the eventual differences in performance between males and females in secondary and tertiary levels of education. Girls are provided structured and repetitive learning experiences in the home, requiring attention to detail, patience and obedience. Boys, on the other hand, are the beneficiaries of male privileging, which relieves them of most of these structured duties while supplying less outside school life-skills training related to realistic adult futures. Thus, girls are better equipped than boys for the highly structured English-framed system of education prevailing in the Caribbean, applying the lessons of their early home training to the exigencies of primary and later school achievement. There is a cruel irony here that the sexism pervading the allocation of household chores leads to long-term gain for girls and the academic under-achievement of boys. The cultural legacy begins in the Cane Piece of the Jamaican household. Jamaican girls are not more intelligent than their brothers; they just have a better preparation in their early years to cope with formal education.

Generating Genius was set up as the 'Cane Piece' for black boys in Britain. By creating a pathway through science to University, we re-engineered that focus on hard work, competition and ambition. We gave our boys the additional education time that was already an aspect of middle-class culture. The programme was akin to the chores that were given to Jamaican girls at 6 years old. The genius would come but it didn't come from the sky. We had to create the right context for it to grow and the context was designed to meet the needs of boys.

Why Science?

Science is a vibrant applied discipline, and because the study of nature is perceived as innate to human identity, science education has a concrete, 'real-world' context to aspire to. This view of 'real' science, as a significant societal process to which science education provides access, presents authenticity – but this was seldom the experience of the boys in their schools.

Educators use inquiry as a dynamic method to demythologise science and enhance learning in a way that avoids the didacticism and intimidation of traditional methods of declarative explanation and rote memorisation. Boys in the UK as well as Jamaica were being bored silly by textbook science. Although men were at the forefront of science, carrying out research for centuries, and consistently dominating the field, much has changed. The present curriculum is more suited to the skills that girls have acquired. It needs to be made exciting for all pupils.

The concept of authenticity has developed various meanings and applications. Bruce is a Jamaican boy who began the programme when he was 11. Now 15 years old, he reflects on its qualities. What is so apparent is how much he loves the authenticity offered by the programme:

> Well, to begin with the Science programme experience gives us a hands-on approach where lab work, procedures and experiments are concerned. In the school system, experiments conducted in laboratories or 'labs' are rare – especially for students at my level (10th grade). During the programme we do a lot of lab work, which is definitely at the more advanced level of Science. The teaching styles of the teachers at school are not as advanced as [those of] our lecturers at UWI. So the programme gives us an advanced approach to the whole field of Science. I like the way we were seen as real scientists and the research we did, like tissue culture (growing plants and fruits in the lab), was linked to reality.

> In Jamaica, there is still considerable difficulty for science to penetrate our people's way of life and become a significant part of the way we're develop-

ing. It is still true that students view sciences as being 'too difficult' or as an area for 'bright people' or 'white male'. I want to keep Science real.

The aspect that stands out the most would be doing, which refers to practical application. This is so because the practical application of what I learn (seeing, listening, reading) is further reinforced. And whatever mistakes I make can be quickly identified and corrected as a result of the practice.

The teaching of the Sciences at my school is excellent but the teachers should try and implement the use of more experiments and lab work so that the teaching can be more effective.

Boys, science and brain power

Research has shown that out-of-school learning of the kind employed by the Generating Genius programme has a strong influence on students' educational outcomes and helps to develop a more positive relationship with science (Shorthand, 1987; Braun and Reiss, 2004). Similarly, research conducted in Jamaican schools has shown that students who were taught by means of a combination of lectures, teacher demonstrations, class discussions and student practical work and in small groups significantly improved in the experimental subjects. Such strategies were used by the Generating Genius programme to get the best out of the boys. And they worked. This is what boys who were on the project said:

There are no words to describe how I feel ... I'm good at these things ... I don't want to end up in the streets doing bad boy things.

The programme has helped me generally with my whole approach to my school work. I have made drastic improvement.

The course has given me a better understanding of robotics and science and has helped to improve my science grade.

The teachers have helped me socially and academically.

I have learned valuable presentation skills; have earned experience with working in the laboratory and practice with social disciplines.

The social programme has helped me to become more confident.

The presentation tasks has helped me to express myself more, developing leadership qualities and team work and making more use of the latest technology.

127

Malcolm Gladwell studied the outcome of affirmative action amongst black students from The University of Michigan Law School. Controversially these students are admitted with slightly lower IQ scores than their white counterparts. According to Gladwell,

> A few years ago, however, the University of Michigan decided to look closely at how the law school's minority students had fared after they graduated. How much money did they make? How far up the profession did they go? How satisfied were they with their careers? What social and community contributions did they make? What kind of honours had they won? They looked at everything that could conceivably be an indication of real-world success. And what they found surprised them. (2008:85)

Gladwell found that there was no discrepancy whatsoever between white students' and black students' achievement. In fact, there were many examples of black students achieving a good deal more than their white classmates.

So can we define what this success factor might be in education terms? If intelligence matters only up to a point, then we need to consider other factors – it has got to be wider than just formal intelligence. These factors emerged in our summer science programmes in the UK.

As the project progressed through the years, other universities became involved: Leeds, Nottingham, Oxford and Brunel in London. There were other activities too, as these students relate.

Two year 11 students aged 15, now in their exam year – call them David and Stephen – give their views on being part of the Generating Genius programme.

David – Setting the horizons high

This summer, I went to two locations for the Generating Genius Programme. The first was the University of Leeds and to tell the truth I wasn't looking too happy about it, because I had came back from Poland the previous night, but nevertheless, I was still up to it. We had gone to Leeds to study cardiovascular sciences and to learn more about the heart and about some of the risks of what can happen to the heart if we don't watch what we do with it. It was very helpful for me, because I had studied the heart before, but not in a lot of detail. I learned things about the heart that I never knew before, and also how to take good care of your heart.

We were asked to come up with a poster campaign, to warn people about the risks of an unhealthy heart. It wasn't something I was particularly nervous about, because I had done it many times so I was up to the challenge. I and my partner Mariam had came up with a poster which was based on the theme of the congestion charge zone, but was adapted to fit the idea that the heart was involved. My group was up against eight or nine other groups, so it was really competitive. But hopefully, our poster did well. We had stayed in Leeds for five days, and it was really interesting. I met new people, tried new things, and went to new places, so it was something new to remember, and what also made the trip memorable was that I had never been to Leeds before, so it was a trip that I will remember for a long time.

After Leeds, I had to go to Brunel University in Uxbridge, West London. Travelling there was the least of my problems. I didn't know my way around the campus, but eventually found my way. We had come to Brunel for a 'zero waste' conference, where we were told to do two things. The first task was to come up with a poster campaign to warn people to stop wasting, and start recycling. The second task was a 'Scrapheap Challenge' style task. We had to build something out of parts from electric toothbrushes, cassette players, computers and, basically, junk. It had to have a theme of zero waste. I found this very challenging because I didn't know what to expect, plus I hadn't done anything like this before, so it was especially challenging for me, but I managed to get on very well, and after listening to the teacher, I was more confident of the task ahead, and I knew what to do.

Halfway into the week, the group I was in was given an extra task: We had to give a presentation on something else related to zero waste. We had to select one subject out of three available. We chose Eco-Schools, so we had to make a campaign to encourage more schools in Britain to 'go green'. We had only three days to do this, but I think that our group worked very well, and the end product was very creditable. Our model however, wasn't as good, but I didn't let it put me down. I was expecting that the final presentations would be held at the University, but then I was told that they were to be held at the Royal Academy of Engineering.

Knowing this gave me time to breathe and to perfect my presentation. When the day came for me to do the presentation, I wasn't feeling nervous at all, because it had come to a point where I had gotten used to the pressure these types of presentations brought. But when I saw how many people had attended, I actually began to feel the nerves, but I managed to calm down. When I was giving my first presentation, I didn't focus on the fact that there were lots of people in the room. The only people I was concentrating on were the judges at the front table. I just tried to speak as loudly and as clearly as I could, explaining all of the facts as quickly but as effectively as I could. As I gave my presentation, my confidence grew and grew, until it came to the point where I didn't care about how many people were in the room. I only cared about giving my presentation.

After I gave my presentation, I was feeling good about myself, so when the time came for me to give my second presentation, I was feeling confident because I knew what to do, and I could also be more creative with what I spoke, and maybe use a little humour here and there to keep the audience's attention. Because I had spent a lot of time on my second presentation, I was determined not to let all this work go to waste, so I began to speak like I did for my other presentations, but this time, I was more open, and more confident and I was even able to add in humour to make the audience interested in what I was saying. So when I found out that I was in a three-way tie for number 1, I was absolutely speechless, but at the same time relieved. I was so relieved that all my work had paid off. Even my dad told me how good I was, so it really made my day.

I had the chance to do various activities during the summer school. In Leeds, I had the chance to practice steel drumming, a little break dancing, creating festival masks, and a few casual activities like a climbing wall. I also got the chance to dissect a pig's heart. That was probably the most exciting part, because I had never seen a real live heart before in real life. It was also a challenge, because cutting up a heart was kind of a gory task, but that was what made it all the better. Leeds was most certainly a new experience because I had the chance to try so many different things, and it helped me to think in new ways that have benefited me a lot. I've never tried steel pan drumming, and I have never break-danced before, so it was a new experience, as well as a tiring one. If I ever had the chance to do that part of the summer school again, I certainly would because I found them very enjoyable, and also I met lots of new people from the Yorkshire area who were funny as well as kind. Everything at Leeds was new, and I think that's why it was such a wonderful time for me, as it gave me time to reflect on who I was, and it made me a better person overall.

In Brunel, it was more the usual stuff that we got to do, like go on the computers, play football, go to the gym, and that sort of stuff. The one thing that I found particularly exciting was the fact that we were doing a 'scrapheap challenge' style task. I had watched Scrapheap Challenge, and I absolutely love it, so I was fairly excited when I learned that we would be doing a similar task. It was a new experience for me because I had always dreamed of doing something like that, and now I have a taste of the types of things that they put up with. The facilities were excellent and the accommodation was superb. I wouldn't mind living in a place like that!! But one thing I didn't like about Brunel was the fact that we had to make our own way there, and it was very nerve-racking, as you didn't know if you were going the right way, until you actually get there. But apart from that, it was very enjoyable.

The social life on campus is very interesting because it is very close to life outside. It has almost everything, and it even looked normal as well. Leeds in particular was very different, because when I arrived at the destination, I thought it was just another road. When I found out that it was part of the university, I was amazed. It looked almost like a normal road, and it made me realise that life on campus was very interesting. I honestly didn't think that a university could look so normal. Brunel, however was much more distinctive, because it looked like a proper university, and you could easily tell it was one when you look at it. But Brunel was also an excellent place to be. It looked so modern, and new, whereas Leeds looked nice, but old at the same time. I can't really compare where was better, because they both had good points and bad points about them, but it gave me a view of what campus life is actually like.

At Generating Genius, I have learnt lots of things, not just science. I have learnt a lot about science, its applications, and how it fits into the world around us. I have also learnt a lot of things about myself that I don't think I would have discovered if I hadn't joined the programme. I have also discovered new skills, and have changed a lot since joining the programme two years ago. All the things I have learnt have really helped me in school, because it means that I have gained an advantage over most of the other students. I have become more confident on the programme, and thus have become more confident at school. I am now more sociable than I was before, and I have a more open mind towards what I want to do in the future.

My favourite moments of the camp were going to Leeds. All of it was a new experience to me. Everything I had done there was unlike anything I had ever done before, and I met new people who were funny as well as fun to be around. If I could ever get the chance to go back there and do it all again, I certainly would. And somehow, it had turned me into a better person, because it gave me time to look at what I wanted to do in life, and where I was looking to go.

My schoolwork is going well, I think. I'm on the way to achieving good grades in August. The subjects I chose to study were ICT, DT and Geography. The things we learnt had helped me a lot, but in ICT and Geography, it couldn't do much for me. It helps a lot in DT though, because it now means that I have acquired new skills that can greatly help me to achieve a better grade when exam time approaches.

Before I came to the course, I only wanted to become a doctor, studying in the medicine fields. But thanks to the programme, it has now widened my eyes, and given me more options as to what I want to do. I am still looking to go to University. That much hasn't changed, but it's now become a question of what it is I want to study in University. I am now torn between Medicine and Engineering, both in the science fields. The reason why I have now considered engineering is because I enjoyed the type of engineering I did at Brunel, and I think I could become very good at it.

Stephen – A boost in motivation

Ever since being on the Generating Genius Programme I have always looked to the summer when we would all meet in order to participate in another research project and this year I was high in anticipation. This summer was split into two parts, with one ending in a final presentation near Central London. The first one was at the University of Leeds, in, of course, Leeds, and the second was at Brunel University, in west London. Both lasted around five days each and were residential, which I thought was great.

The five days in Leeds started at 9am on Monday with an introduction to the course. Over the next few days we built up an understanding of types of cardiovascular disease, in particular coronary heart disease which can lead to angina and is caused by atherosclerosis. Angina is severe pain in the chest because of lack of blood and therefore oxygen supply to the heart and atherosclerosis of the coronary arteries which is when the artery enlarges to try and compensate for the build up of plaque stopping sufficient blood flow. This can eventually lead to the rupture of an artery if the affected area in the artery grows too large. We were taught about the reversible and irreversible risk factors and how it can be prevented, how it starts and develops, and how it is diagnosed.

We also got the chance to take part in two workshops, one where we had to dissect pigs' hearts in order to look closely at the anatomy of a heart and to see exactly where the coronary arteries are and how they are affected. In the other, we gained skills on measuring blood pressure and giving advice on lifestyle changes which we would later use on members of the community in our own clinic. The last two days we used our new found knowledge of cardiovascular diseases to design a health promotion campaign in small groups, which were presented on the last day.

Over these few days I learnt a lot, including some personal information on Wolfe Parkinson White Disease my aunt is suffering from, which gave me a clearer idea as to the cause and also the treatment. For the social activities, we went rock-climbing which although it isn't my favourite thing to do I did enjoy. We also went to a dance class, a carnival costume workshop and a steel drum workshop. Using a steel drum was really exciting to me, probably because I've never used one before then, and, I must say, I was naturally gifted in doing so.

Brunel's five days began with registration at around 8.30am and of course a course overview and an introduction to staff. The objective of these few days would be to look at how we can recycle electronic junk and create something out of scraps that would have a message, it was a task similar to TV's Scrapheap Challenge. We had the rest of our time there to complete this piece with help from H Patten, an artist and design expert, and Steve Thomas, a robotics and engineering expert. But before we got stuck into the scrapheap, we were given a lecture on the 'green agenda' and recycling by Dr Sue Buckingham-Hatfield. The lecture had interesting points about recycling materials at home and turning off appliances we aren't using that I found helpful. After that we had lunch and then were split into to big groups. One group would go to work with the scraps with Steve Thomas, while the other would work on ideas with H Patten or a presentation of a chosen ongoing debate in a computer room.

At around 5pm every day we would get to relax and then do some activities to wind down after working. On the penultimate day we had a lecture that surprised me. It was very intriguing and involving and taught us a lot about presentation skills as well as debating. The last day, we had to present our 'masterpiece' to a Shell representative as well as a Channel 4 news crew, which I think went well. In my opinion, there was more of a social atmosphere at Brunel, probably due to there being a high number of students on campus.

The third part of this summer's session was a final presentation at the Royal Academy of Engineering, where we would present our scrap masterpiece and our presentation on a chosen ongoing debate to a panel and an audience that included our parents. First, when we had finished setting up, the judges came to each pair to ask questions about their model and discuss what it was like making it. Afterwards, the parents and audience were led into the room with the models so they could look at what had been made. Lastly, each pair showed the panel and audience their presentation and advert as best they could. It was all a great evening but it made me wish that the few days we had to do it hadn't been a bit of a rush.

Again, the Generating Genius Programme was a great experience this summer that gives me a boost in motivation to try hard in all my subjects at school, especially after seeing myself on BBC24 and other news channels. This summer has made me thankful I'm on the programme and as usual I'm looking forward to next year.

I'm now in year 11, my second year of GCSEs and it's hard work, as I have to try harder than I did last year with not just school but things other than that. At the moment, I study all three sciences plus English, Maths, Economics, IT, French, Food Technology, Physical Education, PSHE, Citizenship and Religious Studies. I do find all sciences interesting but I enjoy Physics most which is why I'm going to do it for A- level.

Stephen and David were typical of the project, not only in their backgrounds but in their enjoyment of it and their demonstratable rising to its demands. They, like the other boys who were selected, were able – but none of them were considered exceptionally bright. What a challenging but supportive approach to learning can achieve is captured in their accounts. To understand why the programme worked so well for them and the other boys, some of the components are described and analysed, starting with the scrapheap challenge.

The Scrapheap Challenge

We arranged a class of 30 boys into pairs. Their first task was to take an electric toothbrush, open it up, get at the motor, and make it into a spinning object powered by a solar battery. The teacher did a mock demonstration and the students followed. It was a task that all the boys completed with ease. I watched the boys acting like sheep, each carefully taking the brush apart and all coming up with a similar result.

The second exercise really sorted the men from the boys. They were given a limited time to rummage through and collect enough junk from an electronic scrapheap to create a motorised artistic installation that could be exhibited in the Tate Modern art gallery. Initially, there was an enthusiastic rush to collect the junk, although many boys began to lose focus and found the out-of-the-box thinking too much for them. But a significant minority did manage to produce professional style installations.

Gladwell distinguishes the important difference in the two types of exercises:

> [The second] requires you to use your imagination and take your mind in as many different directions as possible. With a divergence test, obviously there isn't a single right answer. What the test giver is looking for are the number and the uniqueness of your responses. And what the test is measuring isn't analytical intelligence but something profoundly different – something much closer to creativity. (2008:91)

The people who were best at doing this were the slave ancestors of most of our boys. During the debrief session, I read to the boys a wonderful piece from Nobel poet Derek Walcott (1998). It summed up not only their genius but also the genius of their Caribbean ancestry:

> Deprived of their original language, the captured and indentured tribes create their own, accreting and secreting fragments of an old, an epic vocabulary, from Asia and from Africa, but to an ancestral, an ecstatic rhythmic in the blood that cannot be subdued by slavery or indenture, while nouns are renamed and the given names of places accepted like Felicity village or Choiseul. (Walcott, 1998:70)

Walcott is saying that certain conditions can bring about genius: now that's where you hit the money: He goes on:

> ... but the process of renaming, of finding new metaphors, is the same process that the poet faces every morning of his working day, making his own tools like Crusoe, assembling nouns from necessity, from Felicity, even renaming himself. (1998:78)

Walcott talks about 'working day': the genius is found in the 'use' and in the doing. Our scrapheap challenge was a great way to bring out that genius. Like Robinson Crusoe facing the challenge to find a way off the island, boys will be able to reach into the storehouse of their imagination and build that boat. Walcott speaks of the need to have some of the old comforts taken away in order to be truly imaginative:

> The stripped man is driven back to that self-astonishing, elemental force, his mind. That is the basis of the Antillean experience, this shipwreck of fragments, these echoes, these shards of a huge tribal vocabulary, these partially remembered customs, and they are not decayed but strong. (Walcott, 1998:67)

The reason the scrapheap challenge was so powerful was that the boys were stripped to their elementals. There was no cut and paste from the internet; these were not mimic men. They were literally taking the old and making it new. This is what their great, great grandparents had to do when they were flung the off-cuts of meat to eat. They turned it into culinary delights such as oxtail stew, cowfoot jelly and tasty pigs' trotters. In the meanwhile, the vegetarian Rastafarians were busy reworking the Bible into their own image and music.

Using the legacy

That teachers hold explicit and implicit stereotypical notions about Black intelligence cannot be denied. Can this however, explain or excuse the failings of black boys in schools? Do teachers share some of the reservations of Hernstein and Murray, authors of *The Bell Curve* (1994), and James Watson? Does this mean they have a low expectation of black students and therefore influence their performance? John McWhorter (2001) challenges this idea and points to cultural factors that exist amongst his fellow African Americans. Ironically, he points to students of Caribbean origin living in America, to show that it is a 'black American problem' and not a 'black' problem, he says:

> There are those who find it very difficult to accept that black American culture, rather than racism and societal inequalities, is the locus of the problem, and there are those who, mostly within the privacy of Internet chat rooms, suspect that all of this simply means that black people are not as intelligent as other ... Yet nothing indicates to me more strongly that both positions are mistaken than the fact that black Caribbeans in America tend strongly not to exhibit this subtle remove from schoolwork ... Thus far, every black undergraduate I have ever taught who has been one of the best students in my class has been of Caribbean extraction. (McWhorter, 2001:144)

McWhorter is right to point to the cultural legacy of intelligence, which puts black Caribbean students in America ahead of their African American peers and well ahead of their black Caribbean cousins in the UK. I have called this the 'Cane Piece' factor. McWhorter's students have an awareness of the tough life of their forebears who had to make great sacrifices for their education, like a cane cutter in Jamaica, who would suffer in the cane field so that he could send his children off to America for a better life.

A decade long study of adult children of immigrants to New York has concluded that they are rapidly entering the mainstream and doing better than their parents in terms of education and earnings – even outperforming native-born Americans in many cases. The results are detailed in *Inheriting the City: The Children of Immigrants Come of Age* (Kasinitz *et al*, 2007)

One important reason given by Kasinitz and colleagues is that even poor, uneducated immigrants have 'shown that they have the drive, ambition, courage and strength to move from one nation to another,' (2007:9) and to transmit their determination to their children. So the second generation is able to take advantage of civil rights programmes, including affirmative action policies, when applying to universities as well as for jobs.

Conquering chemistry

At the age of 12, not only had all the Generating Genius boys learned their Chemistry Periodic table but they understood the concepts, and went on to turn those dry elements into great slam poems. Many of these children were the great-grand children of the Windrush generation that came to the UK from the Caribbean in the 1950s. They are culturally similar to African Americans in that they have little sense of a migrant experience. They are fully embedded in the British context. The programme has broken them away from the culture of underachievement that has beset their peers.

Periodic Table Mnemonic

If you want students to learn the Periodic Table, teach them this Mnemonic:

Harry, Hill, Likes, Boiling, Broth, Chicken, Not, Other, Foods, Naughty, Nick, Made, A, Simple, Pie, Sipping, Chardonnay, And, Katie, Clarkson, Shot, The, Van, Carrying, Many, Farmhouse, Chickens, *and* Nesting, Cinnamon, Zebras. Gaelic, Gangsters, And, Scottish, Break dancers, Keep Rabbits, Shouting, Yodels. Zany, Nervous, Microscopic, Ticks, Run, Radiation, Plants, Across, Cumbria. I, Saw, Sam, Tricking, Ian *and* Xavier, Crouching, Behind, Harlequins, Tied, With, Ropes, On, Inanimate, Pieces. Aliens, Have, Toes, Pressed, By, Potatoes, At, Random, Fractions. Ron, Runs, Diabolical, Scary, Battles, Hence, Many, Underestimating, Underpants, Unanimously.

Their approach to learning was similar to the Greek hero Odysseus's: knowledge acquired for its own sake and applied to find technological solutions to problems. The Periodic Table exercise proves this point: make it into exciting poetry and use it for scientific experiment. Black boys have suddenly become the James Bonds of their generation. They can extricate themselves from danger using their brains as well as their brawn. What brain power does is make sure that the physical energy is tamed. If brawn is going to be used it won't be in any gang warfare but on the side of the female, on the side of things that are positive. At last, our boys are beginning to understand the real nature of self-control.

Transformation in the students was clear to the parents. Comments like these were typical:

> The programme has helped my son tremendously in both his social and academic life. He is more confident and assertive. He is ahead of his classmates academically in most areas.

137

The programme has provided valuable exposure to the field of science in which he is interested and has helped to hone his skills in several areas while helping him to be more focused.

Since becoming a part of the programme he has taken more interest in his academic pursuits. He's now more focused and determined to succeed.

The programme has exposed him to areas that are not covered in the regular school curriculum.

The programme has instilled positive values and attitudes in him; making him more rounded and mature.

The programme has challenged my son and has elevated him from a basic lifestyle of simply doing school assignments because he has to do them to being more focused, inquisitive and willing to do so. From observation I have noticed him challenging himself to remain in the top ten at school by studying very hard and for long hours in order to fight to remain in the Generating Genius Programme. I can say with great pride and joy that this programme has helped in more ways than the ones stated above. It has helped me to not have the difficulty of having to constantly remind him about studying.

The standards are very high and the bar is set high for the boys, hence challenging them and forcing them to work harder. The training received is also good.

The exposure to the many and varied facilities made available to the boys and their ability to work as a team.

Though I am cognizant of the financial constraints, I think the duration of the summer programme could be extended.

The programme needs to become more visible in different communities. As a part of their training the boys should visit children's homes, hospitals and other community service activities.

The Generating Genius programme, a charity, could work only with a small number of boys. However, if there is one thing of which I am convinced and which the case studies in Samoa and Jamaica also strongly confirm, it is that the programme would have been equally effective with a wholly different cohort of boys. It will work in schools and communities everywhere.

Every one of the randomly selected boys who followed the programme went on to pass 9 GCSEs at grade C or above. As the project evolved, we learned what worked best. I hope that by describing our successes and the reasons for them, I have shown how black boys can reverse the spiral of underachievement and become leaders in education and society. That the boys themselves understood what Generating Genius had offered them is apparent from the interview below.

Three of the boys – call them Carlos, Henry and Jack – offer personal and pertinent insights into what our approaches meant to them and why they worked so well. Here they are being interviewed by a 15 year old reporter for the children's newspaper *Headliners*:

Ashleigh: *Did you know that in 2003, 70 per cent of African Caribbean boys left school with less than five GCSEs and the trend has hardly improved?*

Carlos: It's because they lose their ambition and the need to get a good education. In the end they start to rely on the streets and they think they can have a good life on the streets.

Jack: As they grow up they want to be in gangs and they get distracted at school and stop working.

Henry: I agree. They are dragged into the gang business and start to depend on them to get through life. They're not looking to get money through working, they're looking for it the easy way, from the streets.

Ashleigh: *Has the Generating Genius programme really helped you or would you have done well without it?*

Carlos: I was already doing OK at school but the project has shown me what black scientists can achieve and so has helped me to open more doors and has created more career paths for me.

Henry: Before the project I wasn't doing that well in school and I didn't do any work. But now I've seen what I can do. I've seen my potential and I've seen that I could be making money and going into higher places.

Ashleigh: *How did you feel about having to commit to this project for four years? Do you think it was all worthwhile and why?*

Carlos: It's worthwhile because you're not going to change overnight. You could be doing well in the first two years and go into something wrong.

Jack: The project keeps us on track as we're going through school. If it wasn't there then we could fall back and go into something wrong.

Ashleigh: *Why do you think they chose boys and not girls to participate in this scheme, and is it fair?*

Carlos: I think it's because they think black girls are more sensible and black boys are underachieving more. But at the same time they're still both underachieving; if black girls are getting four GCSEs and a black boy is getting three, they're still not making their target of at least getting five.

Jack: Girls find it easier to keep on track.

Henry: Boys are dragged into certain things like fights and they have a reputation and stuff. It's easier for girls, they don't have anything to distract them from school.

Ashleigh: *Do you think role models are important for black boys to have? Do you think having a father at home helps?*

Carlos: Having a father at home would help but to me it doesn't matter as long as I've got my mum.

Jack : I think you should have a role at home, like I've got my mum and mums are good because they cook for you. But I don't think I need a (male) role model, it doesn't make any difference to me.

Ashleigh: *So for you personally you don't need a role model but do you think that black boys in general need role models that are male figures?*

Carlos: Yeah, because when boys look up to their mum they don't learn how to be a man because your mum can't teach you that. That's why male role models come in handy.

Henry: I don't really need a role model because I have grown up just being with my mum. I look up to her because she's motivating me to do this project. One day I will bring home some money and make her proud and it'll be because of all the things she has done for me.

Ashleigh: *Are you doing this scheme to make your parents proud or are you doing this for yourself?*

Jack: I'm doing this for myself and my family because when I have children I don't want to say I was a bin man. I want to say I was a scientist or something and for them to have a good role model instead of them wanting to be a bin man.

Henry: I want to do this for myself so I can look back on it and say 'that was me, I did that. Look how far I got and now I'm in a good job and I've got money.'

Ashleigh: *After seeing other African Caribbean boys in Jamaica striving towards their dreams and becoming high achievers, did it influence you to become more ambitious?*

Carlos: Yeah, they have to work harder to get an education and they have to travel very far to get it. So when I look at them and then look at our kids on the streets here and how they waste their education, when others would die for this opportunity. It just makes me think how grateful I am. I want to go to University do bio-chemistry and set up my own Bio-tech company, then sell it for around a million

Jack: Seeing a black person that's done well in school does make you ambitious. It means you can bring the statistics up and make them better for black boys. I want to go to University to do medicine, make enough money to buy a big house.

What I like most about this interview is that we hear the voice of the boys and the honesty about their experiences. When it comes to race and education, I have been disturbed by how much of the research either ignores the views of the students or asks leading questions until the children confess that they are victims of racism.

The boys speaking here are not naïve. They are aware of a world that will still judge them by the colour of their skin. However nowhere in the interview do they suggest that the reason for black boys failing is due to racism, direct or indirect. They are clear that the matter is more complex but they also recognise that the real barriers exist in the family, the community, peers and within themselves. One politician who should know better once accused me of 'blaming di pickney (children)'. This obsession with white racism is another example of adults taking away the 'Cane Piece' from black boys.

There is no suggestion that these students are undergoing an identity crisis. There seems no conflict in being black and being British. They are aware that black males are positioned negatively by many in the society, but they know it will not stop them from achieving their goals. And Henry made the most telling comment of all when he told *Headliners*: 'Now I've seen what I can do'.

These boys have learned the secret of how to be a genius. They had linked themselves to the same 'Cane Piece' as their Caribbean cousins in America. They would not allow education researchers, self-appointed community leaders or ego driven politicians to tell them that white teachers are their biggest barrier to achievement.

Policy makers in Britain, America and the Caribbean will need to tailor their policies to the complex needs of their boys. This will mean fewer resources devoted to antiracist training, cultural deficit education or bland mentoring schemes. The generating genius methodology provides some key clues in constructing a cultural legacy for these young males. The legacy will provide spaces for vulnerable boys to learn how to respect and take care of each other. In black communities, men have found it hard to acknowledge that they have suffered from poor nurturing. The homophobia police have made the journey towards the feminine that much harder. Equally, a hard nosed feminism that rejects the need for fathers will always result in a generation of young men bound by their raw instincts.

We need to give working-class black boys more hours of schooling, and particularly out of school activities. In places like Jamaica, policy makers may need to think seriously about a national residential youth service for 14 year olds where students would be able to undertake a rites of passage programme of fun, community service, intellectual challenge and sport. Those who object to such direct measures should look to the alternative – that highly efficient social service called violent gangs, which is doing a roaring trade across the black Diaspora.

The story of Generating Genius shows that fostering academic achievement takes thought, effort and time. It shows that one-off interventions rarely work in education. We had to work with our boys over four years. What we gave them was a way of perceiving the world that was rooted in their own Caribbean heritage and which, as Henry said, showed them what they can do. This gave them strength to distance themselves from the negative aspects of peer group pressure and, like great pilots, learn that the sky's the limit.

The lessons for us all
In conclusion, I have tried to set out the principles we followed in the programme in a way that identifies what worked and why. There are ten, but they of course overlap.

■ Boys working together
Research suggests that boys work best when they work together. Jamaica has a strong tradition of single-sex schools and it is these which have produced the country's best leaders and musicians. The usual argument is that boys are distracted in the presence of girls, although

there is little evidence to support this. What has emerged, though, is that boys enjoy working with one another. They long for an all male context where they can freely share with those who have similar experience. Perversely, gangs are now providing this function in a context of crime and violence. Another key characteristic of our project was the social mixing of boys. In Jamaica, we mixed middle class boys with boys from economically poor backgrounds as well as rural and city students. A similar kind of mixture also occurred in the UK.

■ A male friendly curriculum

Boys responded positively to hands-on tasks which had a purpose and a clear outcome. Ironically, science has become regarded as too difficult and as boring. The project used competition as a key motivator. The boys were put into groups and as in the TV's The Apprentice: they elect a project manager and they had a have to complete a specific task. The winner was rewarded; the runners-up encouraged to try again next time.

■ Cultivating the mind over the body

Many of our boys find themselves in situations where the body is 'everything'; in this sense they are under similar pressure to girls. Boys generally see the pursuit of intellectual activity through reading and research as a girl's activity. On the summer camp students as young as 13 were working comfortably at degree level. Mental activity was seen as an enjoyable challenge that they could meet, and kept the distractions of sex and violence in check.

■ Critical thinking, critical engagement

We trained our boys to understand research methodology and practice. It gave them a sense that they had the tools to discover new knowledge. It also helped them to question what knowledge was 'given' and how we question in a rigorous manner. Critical thinking is a key element of the Generating Genius programme. It is taught as a separate subject and is also infused within the science and engineering lessons. Students had to produce their own arguments and analyse those presented by their colleagues. This promoted the higher order thinking skills of analysis, synthesis and evaluation. The tasks demanded self reflection and the ability to think out of the box, a skill which is in big demand in British,

Jamaican, and American organisations. We set up scenarios such as a murder case, linked to our Forensic Science study, which required students to evaluate the strength of evidence and make informed decisions using their critical thinking skills.

■ Perceiving the world through science and the arts

We have tried to move away from the view that science is totally separate from the arts but instead teach our boys that science is an art, with its own discipline and rigour. The use of the imagination is a key space of commonality: suggesting a hypothesis and then testing it is not dissimilar to the crafting of a great poem. When our boys create a power driven artistic installation from a mountain of scrap-electrical junk, they are doing several things at the same time. Not only are they building their knowledge of physics and engineering, but they also have the best lesson imaginable on Caribbean history and culture. They re-make a new world from the scrap elements of the old one. We show them how Bob Marley and St Lucian poet Derek Walcott are Robinson Crusoe style scientists. Once inspired, the boys no longer see science as difficult or boring but as every bit as interesting as making a song or crafting a fascinating story.

■ Positive attitudes to males

The programme assumed a high degree of maturity in the participants. We treated 13 year old schoolboys as if they were 18 year old university students. We set the bar high, not only academically but emotionally. It also means that teachers show respect and do not undermine the intelligence of the boys. We assumed that the boys themselves have innate intelligence which we adults could learn from, and this creates a learning community.

■ Relevant lessons with real and evident purpose

In many developed countries, pupil attitudes to school science decline during secondary schooling and progressively fewer students are choosing to study science at higher levels and as a career. Responses to these developments have included proposals to reform the curriculum, pedagogy, and the nature of pupil discussion in science lessons. We support such changes but argue that far greater use needs to be made of out-of-school sites to make science education more valid and more motivating. Our contention is that laboratory-based school science teaching needs to be complemented by out-of-school science learning that draws on the actual world (through fieldtrips), the presented world (in science centres, botanic gardens, zoos and science museums), and the virtual worlds that are increasingly available through communication technologies.

Our boys learned certain key social and emotional skills through their engagement in high level science and technology. We recognised that young boys love hands on activity, competition and purpose, so we tackled robotics, forensic science, green technology, genetic engineering, nano-technology, video-game software writing, building FM radios, making amplifiers for MP3 players from scrap electronics, constructing solar driven power boats and much more.

■ Emotional development
Given the vulnerable context in which boys are positioned in Jamaica and the UK, programmes and interventions should incorporate planned emotional support for students. Lack of maturity and resilience can be addressed by putting the boys into contexts where they are given challenges on a number of levels. However, this inevitably produces some raw emotional cold turkey withdrawal and this demands regular personal and group talking therapy. We employed counsellors to support the boys on their emotional odyssey towards manhood.

■ Social skills
We taught our boys the art of fine dining and social etiquette – not for them to become quaint or elitist, but because too many are underexposed to wider contexts. They learned how to network and acquired the rituals needed to be a 'gentleman'. They become leaders in conflict management and masters in avoiding violence and retaining their dignity. And they had to undertake 'Community service' by giving back to younger children what they themselves have been taught.

■ A journey to manhood
Masculinity and male initiation rites that signify maturity are defined in every culture by being non-feminine. Much of the Generating Genius energy is really a journey of discovery, where boys not only break from

over-mothering but also find a healthy female side, learning compromise, nurturing skills, verbal presentation skills, and how to manage their egos. There are high risks in this but any rites of passage must entail risk. As Reggae singer Dennis Brown once sang: 'A man must go through tribulation to know himself'. So the boys follow a community service programme, physical exercise and leadership training.

Conclusion

The Generating Genius programme revealed that doing well academically has little to do with innate genius. It suggests a prosaic, democratic, even puritanical view of the world. The key factor that distinguishes geniuses from the merely accomplished is not a divine spark. It's not IQ, a generally poor predictor of success, even in realms like chess. Instead, it's persistent practice. Top performers spend many more hours than others rigorously practicing their craft. If African American and African Caribbean boys watch more television than any other group (and not the Discovery Channel) then providing them with engaging intellectual alternatives will surely improve on their exam grades.

So genius needs to be seen less as a special gift and rather as linked to cultural legacy. What Mozart had, we now believe, was the same quality as Tiger Woods: the ability to focus for long periods of time, plus a father intent on giving his son the protective lawlines. Mozart played a lot of piano at a very young age, so he got his 10,000 hours of practice in early and built from there.

We worked with a group of boys for around four years, following our principles of surrounding them with ritual, love and schooling. And all the boys excelled, even in schools and social contexts that were not supportive of great academic prowess. This is immensely empowering but at the same time tragic. It means that the black diaspora is teaming with potential Barack Obamas but is instead witnessing the waste and loss of so much talent. Schools and the wider society will continue to practice racism and the streets of London, New York and Kingston will provide great peer pressure and danger for vulnerable males. Generating Genius, through its unique methods, has shown that we can, however, provide for most black boys a solid path to success.

References

Allen, S. M. and Hawkins, A. J. (1999) Maternal gatekeeping: Mothers' beliefs and behaviour that inhibit greater father involvement in family work. *Journal of Marriage and the Family* 61: 199-212

Bateson, G., Jackson, D., Haley, J. and Weakland J.H. (1956) Towards a theory of Schizophrenia. *Behavioural Science*, 1 (4) [reprinted in Bateson, G. *Steps to an Ecology of Mind*. London: Paladin, 1973]

Bianchini, J.A. and Colburn, A. (2000) Teaching the nature of science through inquiry to prospective elementary teachers: A tale of two researchers. *Journal of Research in Science Teaching*, 37: 177-209

Booth A, Amato P.R. (2001) Parental predivorce relations and offspring postdivorce well-being *Journal of Marriage and the Family* 63(1): 197-212

Boszormenyi-Nagy, I. and Spark, G. (1973) *Invisible Loyalties: Reciprocity in Intergenerational Family Therapy.* Hagerstown, Maryland: Harper and Row

Bowlby, J. (1973) *Attachment and Loss Vol II: Separation, Anxiety and Anger.* London: The Hogarth Press

Brand, M. and Reiss, M. (2004) The nature of learning sciences outside the classroom. In M. Brand and M. Reiss (eds) *Learning science outside the classroom*, London: Routledge/Falmer

Britton, R. (1989) The Missing link; parental sexuality in the Oedipus Complex, in J. Steiner (ed) *The Oedipus Complex Today: Clinical Implications*, London: Karnac

Brown, J. and McGarrity, G. (1997) *Gender and the young Child: A Jamaican community exploration*, Washington DC: World Bank

Byfield, C (2008) *Black Boys Can Make It – how they overcome the obstacles to university in the UK and USA* Stoke on Trent: Trentham

Cabrera, N.J., Tamisk-LeMonda, C.S., Bradley, R.H, Hofferth, S. and Lamb, M.E. (2000) Fatherhood in the twenty-first century, *Child Development* 71: 127-136

Chevannes, B. (2001) *Learning to be a man*, Kingston, University of the West Indies Press

Cobern, W. (1996) Contextual constructivism, culture in the learning and teaching of science, in Western Michigan Scientific Literacy and cultural studies.

Cooper, C (2008) 'Young Men Afraid to Succeed' in the *Jamaican Gleaner*, 2 November

Crouch, S (1995) *The All-American Skin Game*, New York, Random House

Dhondy, F (1999) 'Institutional Racism' *Times Educational Supplement* Feb 19 p9

Dowling, E. and Gorrell Barnes, G. (2000) *Working with Children and Parents through Separation and Divorce,* Basingstoke: Macmillan.

Dunn, J, Cheng, H., O'Connor, T. G. and Bridges, L. (2004) Children's perspectives on their relationships with their nonresident fathers: influences, outcomes and implications. *Journal of Child Psychology and Psychiatry* 45 (3): 553-566

Eldredge, J (2001) *Wild at Heart: Discovering the Secrets of a Man's Soul,* Nashville: Thomas Nelson

Etchegoyen, A. (2002) Psychoanalytical ideas about fathers, in Trowell, J. and Etchegoyen, A. (eds) (2002) *The Importance of Fathers: A psychoanalytic re-evaluation* Hove: Brunner Routledge

Falk, J, Coulson, D, and Mouussouri, T. (1998) The effect of visitor's agenda on museum learning, *Curator* 41(2): 106-120

Feldman, R. (2003) Infant-Mother and Infant-Father Synchrony: The Coregulation of Positive Arousal, *Infant Mental Health Journal,* 24(1); 1-23.

Figueroa, M. (1996) Male Privileging and Male Academic Performance in Jamaica. Symposium paper with Sudhanshu Handa, Centre for Gender and Development Studies, UWI St. Augustine

Fonagy, P. and Target, M. (1997) Attachment and reflective function: their role in self- organisation. *Development and Psychopathology,* 9: 679-700

Fordham, S. (1996) *Blacked Out: dilemmas of Race, Identity and Success at Capital High,* University of Chicago Press

Fordham, S. and Ogbu, J. U. (1986) Black students' school success: Coping with the 'burden of 'acting White.' *The Urban Review,* 18(3): 176-206

Fout, J. and Tantillo, M. (1993) (eds) *American sexual politics: sex, gender and Race since the civil war,* University of Chicago Press

Freud, S. (1920) 'Identification', in *The Standard Edition of the Complete Psychological Works of Sigmund Freud, vol XVIII,* London: The Hogarth Press 1955.

Frosh, S., Phoenix, A. and Pattman, R. (2001) *Young Masculinities: Understanding Boys in Contemporary Society,* London: Palgrave

Gilmore, D.D .(1990) *Manhood in the Making: Cultural Concepts of Masculinity.* New Haven: Yale University Press

Gilroy, P. (2000) *Between Camps,* Harmondsworth: Penguin

Ginzburg, R. (1988) *100 years of Lynching,* Baltimore: Black Classic

Gladwell, M (2008) *Outliers: the Story of Success,* New York: Allen Lane

Greenson, R. (1968) Disidentifying from mother: its special importance for the boy, *International Journal of Psychoanalysis* 49: 370-374

Grossmann, K., Grossmann, K. E., Fremmer-Bombik, E., Kindler, H., Scheurer-Englisch, H., and Zimmermann, P. (2002) The uniqueness of the child-father attachment relationship: Fathers' sensitive and challenging play as a pivotal variable in a 16-year long study. *Social Development,* 11: 307-331.

Haley, J. (1976) *Problem-Solving Therapy,* New York: Harper and Row

Harris, M. (1993) 'The evolution of human gender hierarchies: a trial formulation', in (ed) B. Miller, *Sex and Gender Hierarchies,* (ed) England: Cambridge University Press

Hart, R (2002) *Slaves who abolished Slavery: Blacks in Rebellion,* University of the West Indies Press

Herrnstein, R. J. and Murray, C. (1994) *The Bell Curve: Intelligence and class structure in American Life,* New York: Free Press

Hewlett, B. S. (1992) Husband-wife reciprocity and the Father-Infant Relationship among Aka Pygmies, in (ed.) B S Hewlett, *Father-Child Relations: Cultural and Biosocial Contexts,* New York: Aldine de Gruyter

Hinde, R. (1982) *Ethology: Its Nature and Relations with Other Sciences,* Glasgow: Fontana

Hobson, R.P., Patrick, M.P.H., Crandell, L.E., Garcia Pérez, R.M. and Lee, A. (2004) Maternal sensitivity and infant triadic communication. *Journal of Child Psychology and Psychiatry,* 45 (3): 470-480

148

REFERENCES

Hodes, M. (1997) *White women, Black Men: Illicit sex in the nineteenth century south*, New Haven: Yale University Press

Homer (2003) *The Odyssey*, Penguin Classics, 2003 edition

Horwood, M. and Fergusson, J. (1998) *Pediatrics* 101 (1) January 1998 p 1-9

Hudson, L. and Jacot, B. (1991) *The way men think: Intellect intimacy and the erotic imagination*, New Haven: Yale University Press

Hutton, C. (1999) 'The Gyalification of Man: The Expression of Male-Male Conflict in Jamaica and the Roots of Homoeroticism in the Political Ideology, Ontology and Praxis of White Supremacy'. Paper presented at CSA, Panama City

Jaffee S.R., Moffitt T.E., Caspi A. and Taylor A. (2003) Life With (or Without) Father: The Benefits of Living with Two Biological Parents depend on the Father's Antisocial Behavior, *Child Development,* 74 (1): 109-126

Jalmert, L. (1990) 'Increasing men's involvement as fathers in the care of children', in *Men as Carers for Children*. Brussels: European Commission Childcare Network

Jordan, W. (1974) *The White Man's Burden*, Oxford: Oxford University Press

Kasintz, P, Mollenkopf, J, Waters, M, Holdaway, J. (2007) *Inheriting the City: The Children of Immigrants Come of Age*, Harvard University Press

Kelly, J.B. (2000) Children's adjustment in conflicted marriage and divorce: a decade review of research, *Journal of the American Academy of Child and Adolescent Psychiatry*, 39: 963-973

Kindlon, D and Thompson, M (1999) *Raising Cain,* London: Michael Joseph

Kraemer, S. (2000) The Fragile Male, *British Medical Journal*, 321: 1609-1612

Lamb M. E. and Lewis C. (2004) The Development and Significance of Father-Child Relationships in two-Parent Families, in M. E. Lamb (ed) *The Role of the Father in Child Development* (fourth edition) Hoboken NJ: Wiley

Leff, J. and Vaughn, C. (1985) *Expressed Emotion in Families: Its Significance for Mental Illness.* New York: Guilford Press.

Main, M. and Hesse, E. (1990) Parents' unresolved traumatic experiences are related to infant disorganised attachment status; Is frightened and/or frightening parental behavior the linking mechanism? In M Greenberg, D. Cicchetti, E.M. Cummings (eds) *Attachment in the Preschool Years*. University of Chicago Press

McDougall, J. (1989) *Theatres of the Body,* London: Free Association Books

McWhorter, J. (2000) *Losing the Race: Self-Sabotage in Black America,* New York: Simon and Schuster

Millar, R. and Osbourne, J. (1998) Nuffield Seminars: Unpublished Interim Report

Minuchin, S. (1974) *Families and Family Therapy.* London: Tavistock

Morrell, J and Murray, L. (2002) Infant and Maternal Precursors of Conduct Disorder and Hyperactive Symptoms in Childhood: A Prospective Longitudinal Study from 2 Months to 8 Years, *Journal of Child Psychology and Psychiatry*, 43(7): 1-20

Neall, L (2007) *About Our Boys: a practical guide to bringing out the best in boys,* London: Neall Scott Partnerships UK

Oyeku, S. (2003) A closer look at racial disparities in breastfeeding. Commentary on breastfeeding advice given to African American and white women by physicians and WIC counsellors in *Public Health Rep 2003* No 101, 118(4): 377-8

Palazzoli, M. S, Boscolo, L., Cecchetti, G. and Prata, G. (1978) *Paradox and Counterparadox*, New York: Jason Aronson.

Patrick, M., Hobson, R.P., Castle, D., Howard, R. and Maughan, B. (1994) Personality disorder and mental representation of early social experience, *Development and Psychopathology,* 6: 375-388

Phillips, A. (1993) *Trouble with Boys.* London: Pandora

Pruett, K.D. (1993) The paternal presence, *Families in Society: Journal of Contemporary Human Services,* 74 (1): 46 –50

Rahm, J. (2002) Emergent learning opportunities in an inner-city gardening program, *Journal of Research in Science Teaching* 39 (2): 164-184

Redfearn, J. (1992) *The Exploding Self: The Creative and Destructive Nucleus of the Personality.* Wilmette, Illinois: Chiron Publications

Rodgers, J.A. (1970) *Sex and Race: Negro-Caucasian Mixing in All Ages and All Lands: The Old World,* Helga M. Rogers USA, Studies in Imperialism

Roth, W. (1997) From everyday science to science education. How science and technology inspired curriculum design and classroom research. *Science and Education* 6: 360-370

Russell, G. and Radojevic, M. (1992) The changing role of fathers? Current understanding and future directions for research and practice, *Infant Mental Health Journal,* 13(4): 296-311

Shortland, M. (1987) No business like show business, *Nature* 328: 213-214

Steele, H., Steele, M., and Fonagy, P. (1996) Associations among attachment classification of mother, fathers, and their infants, *Child Development,* 67: 541-555

Steele, H and Steele, M (2004) The construct of coherence as an indicator of attachment security in middle childhood: The friends and family interview. In K. Kerns, and R. Richardson (eds) *Attachment in Middle Childhood.* New York: Guilford Press

Stone, L. and Bolt, G. (eds) (1994) *The Education feminism reader,* London: Routledge

Target, M. and Fonagy, P. (2002) The role of the father, in J. Trowell and A. Etchegoyen (eds) *The Importance of Fathers: A psychoanalytic re-evaluation,* Hove: Brunner Routledge

Trevarthen, C. and Aitken, K.J. (2001) Infant Intersubjectivity: Research, Theory and Clinical Applications. *Journal of Child Psychology and Psychiatry,* 42: 3-48

Von Klitzing, K., Simoni H. and Bürgin, D. (1999) Child Development and early triadic relationships. *International Journal of Psychoanalysis,* 80: 71- 89

Walcott, D. (1998) *What the Twilight Says,* London: Faber and Faber

Whitaker, C. (1977) Symbolic Sex in Family Therapy. reprinted in J. R. Neill and D.P. Kniskern (eds) *From Psyche to System: The Evolving Therapy of Carl Whitaker.* New York: Guilford Press, 1982

White L. (1999) Contagion in family affection: Mothers, fathers, and young adult children, *Journal of Marriage and the Family* 61 (2): 284-294

Winnicott, D.W. (1960) The Theory of the Parent-Infant Relationship, International Journal of Psycho-Analysis 41: 585-595, reprinted in *The Maturational Processes and the Facilitating Environment,* London: The Hogarth Press,1965, p 37-55

Index